People Patterns

People Patterns

*A Modern Guide
to the
Four Temperaments*

Stephen Montgomery, Ph.D.

 © Archer Publications 2002

Printed in the United States of America
First Edition

ISBN 1-885705-03-4

Contents

...our purpose... is to recognize each other,
to learn to see the other and honor him for what he is.

—Hermann Hesse

Introduction

Try To See It My Way

In 1965 the Beatles sang,

> Try to see it my way—do I have to keep on talking till I can't go on?

And two years later they returned to the same theme:

> You say "yes," I say "no," you say "stop," and I say "go, go, go."

In many ways the Beatles had their fingers on the pulse of their times, and both of these early songs touched on a new attitude that was changing the way people looked at each other in England, the United States, and much of Europe. The button-down, homogenized 1950s had given way to the "do your own thing" 60s, and many people, especially young people, were beginning to understand that human beings are not all alike. The new saying among the rock-and-roll generation was "different strokes for different folks," although some mainstream voices in American popular culture were beginning to express the same idea—Frank Sinatra recorded "My Way" in 1968, Sammy Davis, Jr. released "I've Gotta Be Me" in 1969, Barbra Streisand starred in and sang the title song from "The Way We Were" in 1973, and (would you believe) Burger King launched its "Have It Your Way" ad campaign in 1974.

Now, the aim of scientists is to make sense of the world by finding order in chaos, that is, by discerning categories or patterns in what appears to be the randomness of nature. And so some in medicine and psychology began trying to identify areas of common ground in people's personalities and lifestyles—looking to discover and to map islands, even continents, of similarity in the seas of 60s' diversity.

1

One approach, and it has continued to this day, was to split everyone into two large camps. Are you a "Type A" or a "Type B" personality? Are you "left brained" or "right brained"? Are you from Venus or Mars?

Divisions like these have the virtue of simplicity, and over the years they have caught on pretty well in the public's imagination. But the trouble is, there are so many people who don't fit into either category, or who fit only part of the time. There are "right brain" academics who aren't in the least neat and tidy. Einstein, for example. There are unmistakably feminine Venusian women who are also tough-minded and aggressive. Think of the rock star Madonna. And there are "Type A" workaholics who are free and easy in their personal lives. Remember Bill Clinton?

At the other end of the spectrum, a number of highly intricate systems for typing personality styles have been devised since the 1960s. Don Richard Riso, for example, writes about an ancient Sufi nine pointed star, the Enneagram (first introduced into the U.S. in the early 1970s), that identifies nine personality types, each having nine possible levels of development. And Isabel Myers and Katheryn Briggs created an elaborate questionnaire, *The Myers Briggs Type Indicator* (published in book form in 1962), that distinguishes between sixteen separate personality types, each made up of four independent elements of personality, reflecting a person's "dominant," "auxiliary," "tertiary," and "inferior" mental functions, with each part shadowed by its opposite.

Personality types, however, don't have to be either oversimplified or overcomplicated in this way. Right around 1960 David Keirsey began exploring the idea that people come in four basic models. Studying the Myers materials, Keirsey recognized four clear, strong patterns of personality in Myers's sixteen type portraits, and he connected this to the idea of the "four temperaments" that physicians, philosophers, and poets had been talking about since the time of Hippocrates, around 370 B.C. And so in the late 1970s, after years of teaching and counseling with the temperament model, Keirsey wrote up his ideas in *Please Understand Me*, a practical, non-academic little book that found a huge audience and soon became a best seller.

Please Understand Me managed to strike just the right balance in the field of personality theory. On the one hand it was simple enough to grasp without a graduate degree; and on the other hand it was well founded, tapping into what was for over two thousand years the commonly accepted view of human nature.

Then in 1998 Keirsey thoroughly revised and expanded his ideas in *Please Understand Me II*, spelling out in much greater detail the nature, the history, and the theoretical basis of the four temperaments. No question, *Please Understand Me II* tells you everything you wanted to know about the four temperaments—and maybe more. A Ph.D. (and Professor Emeritus) in psychology, but also a lifelong student of philosophy and political/military history, Keirsey poured twenty years of research and rethinking into his new book. And while *Please Understand Me II* is now the leading work in temperament studies, with one reviewer calling it "the definitive book on temperament," it can be a little daunting in both content and vocabulary.

Which brings me to the purpose of this book. My goal is to make Keirsey's recent ideas on the four temperaments more accessible to people who just want an introduction to temperament theory, a guidebook that's concise and easy to read, and that draws on popular entertainment—music, stories, movies, TV—for its examples. To put it simply, I want to help people understand and have some fun with *Please Understand Me II*.

After working closely with Dr. Keirsey for more than twenty years, as both his editor and research assistant, I'm convinced that learning about the four temperaments can help people in all of the most important parts of their lives—in their marriages, in their role as parents, and in their choice of careers. But first people need to develop what I like to call Foursight, or the ability to see these four basic patterns of personality—Keirsey's four temperaments—both in themselves and in the people near and dear to them.

Or as the Beatles put it in another great song, both "within you and without you."

3

1

Sorting Things Out

Upon arriving at Hogwarts school for wizards, and before sitting down to the welcoming banquet, Harry Potter and all the other first year students (in J.K. Rowling's marvelous series of *Harry Potter* novels) are asked to take part in the serious and scary business of the Sorting Ceremony.

An ancient wizard's hat, patched and frayed, is placed upon a four-legged stool in the middle of the school's Great Hall. This is the Sorting Hat, and each new student is called, one by one, to approach the stool and put on the hat. The Sorting Hat is magically alive, you see, and its job is to listen to each student's thoughts for a few moments, trying to catch the note of his or her true nature, and then to call out, through a tear near the brim, which of the four residence houses the student will call home. Each house at Hogwarts has its own noble history and its own unique character—almost exactly fitting the four temperaments, by the way (see below, pg. 15)—and the Sorting Hat makes sure that the personality of the student and the character of the house are well suited to each other.

Now I also think it best to start with a sorting ceremony...of sorts. Readers will get a lot more out of this book if they begin by taking the time to find out their own temperament style. Harry Potter found that belonging to one of the four Hogwarts' houses gave him a sense of pride in his own personality, and a strong camaraderie with his housemates, not to mention setting up a (mostly) friendly rivalry with the other three houses.

And while I don't have a magical hat that can read minds and identify temperaments, I do recommend spending a few minutes answering the following questions in a new, short-form version of *The Keirsey Temperament Sorter*, the most widely used personality inventory in the world.

The Montgomery Shorter Sorter

Decide on answer **a** or **b** and put a check mark next to the question number on the answer form on pg. 8. Scoring directions and a sample answer form are provided. There are no right or wrong answers since about half the population agrees with whatever answer you choose. If both answers seem to fit you, try to pick the one that appealed to you on first thought. Please answer all the questions.

1 In company do you tend to

__(a) start up conversations   __(b) wait to be approached

2 Do you live more in

__(a) the world as it is   __(b) the realm of possibility

3 Do you more often see things

__(a) with your eyes wide open   __(b) in your mind's eye

4 When dealing with others do you try to be

__(a) firm and objective   __(b) gentle and sympathetic

5 In discussions do you care more about

__(a) making good arguments   __(b) finding points of agreement

6 As a job wraps up do you want to

__(a) tie up all the loose ends   __(b) start on something else

7 Do you typically

__(a) make up your mind quickly   __(b) consider at some length

8 In a new job or class do you tend to

__(a) make friends easily   __(b) keep more to yourself

9 Would you call yourself more

__(a) practical   __(b) theoretical

10 To solve problems do you rely more on

__(a) common sense   __(b) your own analysis

11 Are you more comfortable giving people

__(a) honest criticism   __(b) approval and encouragement

12 Do you base your decisions more on

__(a) impersonal data   __(b) personal wishes

13 Do you find that schedules

__(a) give needed structure   __(b) are too restrictive

14 Would you rather be seen as

__(a) constant   __(b) unpredictable

15 At parties do you like to

__(a) meet and chat with everyone   __(b) enjoy a few close friends

16 Do you more often feel

__(a) in touch with your surroundings   __(b) lost in thought

17 Facts

__(a) speak for themselves   __(b) suggest principles

18 Are you more inclined to be

__(a) cool and collected   __(b) warm and enthusiastic

19 In evaluating others are you usually

__(a) frank and straightforward   __(b) friendly and considerate

20 Going on vacation, do you prefer to

__(a) make plans in advance   __(b) go where the road leads you

21 Are you happier

__(a) getting things settled   __(b) exploring alternatives

22 Does being with groups of people tend to

__(a) energize you   __(b) wear you out

23 Are you better at

__(a) noticing important details   __(b) seeing the big picture

24 Childhood is best spent developing

__(a) physical and social skills   __(b) worlds of make-believe

25 Which do you admire more in others:

__(a) strength of will __(b) strength of feeling

26 Which rules you more:

__(a) your head __(b) your heart

27 Is a mess something you usually

__(a) want straightened up __(b) can live with

28 Do you tend to spend money

__(a) pretty carefully __(b) more on impulse

29 Do you think of yourself as

__a) outgoing and expressive __(b) private and reserved

30 Are you more of a

__(a) nuts and bolts sort of person __(b) fanciful sort of person

31 Are you more likely to trust

__(a) your experiences __(b) your insights

32 Do you consider yourself

__(a) tough-minded __(b) sentimental

33 Which do you value more in yourself:

__(a) being reasonable __(b) being devoted

34 Would you say you are more

__(a) definite and determined __(b) casual and easygoing

35 Do you feel better about

__(a) coming to closure __(b) keeping your options open

36 Do you prize in yourself

__(a) a strong grasp of reality __(b) a complex imagination

37 Are you swayed more by

__(a) convincing evidence __(b) a touching appeal

38 Do you prefer to

__(a) plan your free time __(b) just see what turns up

Answer Form

Enter a check for each answer in the column for **a** or **b**.

	a	b		a	b		a	b		a	b		a	b		a	b		a	b
1			2			3			4			5			6			7		
8			9			10			11			12			13			14		
15			16			17			18			19			20			21		
22			23			24			25			26			27			28		
29			30			31			32			33			34			35		
			36						37						38					

E I **S N** **T F** **J P**

or or

Directions for Scoring

1. Count down each column and write the **a** and **b** scores in the boxes indicated by the arrows. Note that for the columns ending in 36, 37, and 38, you'll bring the scores down and write them in the lower boxes to the right. (See the next page for an illustration.)

2. The first set of **a** and **b** scores is already totalled in the **E I** box. Now add up the two sets of scores in the stacked boxes and write the totals into the boxes marked **S N**, **T F**, and **J P**.

3. You now have four pairs of scores. Circle the letter below the larger score for each pair, **E** or **I**, **S** or **N**, **T** or **F**, **J** or **P**.

4. Finally, look at the letters **S** and **N**. These are your temperament anchor letters. Select the one you've circled and, following the arrows, bring it down and write it in one of the large boxes centered below. Bring down only <u>one</u> letter. If your letter is **S**, check your **J P** scores and write whichever letter is circled next to the **S**. If your letter is **N**, check your **T F** scores and write whichever letter is circled next to the **N**. Put a large X in the box that remains blank.

Sample Answer Form

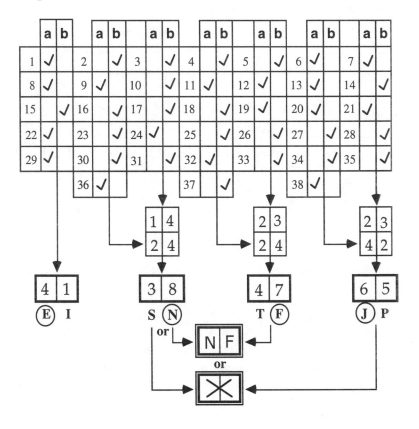

Temperaments and Types

Your temperament is indicated by the two letters written in one of the large boxes at the bottom of the answer form. You should be an **SP**, an **SJ**, an **NF**, or an **NT**. This temperament is the home base of your personality, and you'll find a complete portrait in Chapter 2. Your individual personality type is indicated by the four circled letters; you can find your type listed below, and you can read your type portrait in the Appendix at the end of this book.

In case you're wondering what the letters stand for, I discuss them briefly in the next few pages. But because remembering all the letters and meanings can get confusing, I'll refer to the temperaments and types throughout the rest of this book by the following descriptive names coined by David Keirsey in *Please Understand Me II*:

SP = Artisan	**SJ = Guardian**
ESTP = Promoter	ESTJ = Supervisor
ISTP = Crafter	ISTJ = Inspector
ESFP = Performer	ESFJ = Provider
ISFP = Composer	ISFJ = Protector
NF = Idealist	**NT = Rational**
ENFJ = Teacher	ENTJ = Fieldmarshal
INFJ = Counselor	INTJ = Mastermind
ENFP = Champion	ENTP = Inventor
INFP = Healer	INTP = Architect

What the Letters Mean

The letter names of the sixteen types ("ENFJ," for example) are assembled from four pairs of letters—E or I, S or N, T or F, J or P—most of which stand for concepts introduced by Carl Jung in his book *Psychological Types* (1921). In the 1950s Isabel Myers took up Jung's work on personality, added the J-P scale herself, and developed a questionnaire and a remarkable series of sixteen descriptive portraits that generated worldwide interest in personality types.

In the Myers-Briggs system, the letters stand for the following elements of personality:

E = **Extraversion**   or   **I** = **I**ntroversion
S = **S**ensation   or   **N** = i**N**tuition
T = **T**hinking   or   **F** = **F**eeling
J = **J**udging   or   **P** = **P**erceiving

Myers's idea was to pose a series of questions that weigh these alternatives, and then to piece together a personality type out of the responses. For instance, someone whose answers indicate Introversion, Sensation, Feeling, and Judging is an **ISFJ**, while someone preferring Extraversion, iNtuition, Thinking, and Perceiving is an **ENTP**. And so on, through all the sixteen combinations.

Using the Jung/Myers words to describe the four temperaments, **SP**s can be thought of as **S**ensation-**P**erceiving, **SJ**s as **S**ensation-**J**udging, **NF**s as i**N**tuitive-**F**eeling, and **NT**s as i**N**tuitive-**T**hinking.

What the Words Mean

Unfortunately, not only are some of the Jung/Myers words hard to understand in themselves, they also seem to get in each other's way. What is "Sensation," for instance, and just how is it different from "Feeling"? Or, what is "Intuition," and exactly how does it differ from "Perceiving"? To try to clarify what these words mean, here are some practical definitions:

• **Extraversion** and **Introversion** are terms familiar to most people. Those with strong Extraversion have a more outgoing, gregarious, and talkative social style, while those tending to Introversion are more quiet, retiring, and reserved.

• **Sensation** and **Intuition** are more difficult terms, but since they anchor the four temperament descriptions, it's important we get them straight. Very simply, those strong in Sensation pay more attention to what's going on outside themselves in the concrete world of solid objects and real-world experiences. Those given to iNtuition pay more attention to what's going on inside themselves in the abstract world of ideas and concepts, theories and imaginings.

• **Thinking** and **Feeling** indicate how people govern themselves and deal with others. Those strong in Thinking will more often use

11

their head to rule themselves and their relationships, while those given to Feeling will more often follow their heart.

• **Judging** and **Perceiving** indicate how people make decisions and arrange their lives. Those strong in Judging tend to make up their mind quickly and want to run things according to schedules. Those given to Perceiving tend to put off final decisions, preferring to keep their schedules flexible and their options open.

Different Strokes...

But there's another problem. Because the Jung/Myers words stand for such broad concepts, they tend to blur important differences among the temperaments.

You see, the anchor word "Sensation" suggests something significantly different for Artisans (SPs) than it does for Guardians (SJs). Artisans certainly want to experience strong sensations, and some like to create a sensation wherever they go. But what's more important to understand about the Artisans is that they want their sensations always to be new, exciting, and spur-of-the-moment, and so a more accurate word for them is Spontaneous. On the other hand, for Guardians the notion of "sense" means something altogether different, something closer to "levelheadedness," as in having "common sense," or showing "good sense," and so they are better thought of as Sensible people.

In much the same way, the anchor word "iNtuition" names a strong suit of Idealists (NFs), but it doesn't apply to Rationals (NTs) all that well, at least not in the ordinary meaning of the word, something along the lines of "a feeling in one's bones." The American Heritage dictionary actually defines "intuition" as "knowing or sensing without the use of rational processes," and so the word misdescribes most Rationals right off the bat. Rationals want to know everything that's useful to them, but they rely far more on rational processes—analyzing data, making logical deductions, designing experiments, etc.—than on some sort of mysterious sixth sense, and so they are much better described as iNgenious people.

And it's the same with the supporting cast of words. "Perceiving" and "Judging" on the one hand, and "Feeling" and "Thinking" on the other, are such general terms that they capture very little of the unique character of the four temperaments. If we could choose new, temperament-specific words, Artisans might better be thought of as **P**layful in their perceptions; Guardians as **J**udicious in their judgments; Idealists as **F**ervent in their feelings; and Rationals as **T**heoretical in their thinking.

The bottom line is that, in order to describe the four temperaments more accurately, and also to bring them alive and give them some personality, we need to take a new look at the Jung/Myers letters and the words they stand for:

> **Artisans (SPs):** **S**pontaneous and **P**layful
>
> **Guardians (SJs):** **S**ensible and **J**udicious
>
> **Idealists (NFs):** i**N**tuitive and **F**ervent
>
> **Rationals (NTs):** i**N**genious and **T**heoretical

For those readers familiar with the Jung/Myers terminology, and who use the Myers-Briggs letters as a personality type shorthand, these new words are much closer to giving a clear sense of Keirsey's four temperaments.

The Temperament Matrix

But let's face it: general or specific, accurate or inaccurate, new or old, all of these letters and words are hard to remember and to keep straight. So let's turn now to a different way of sorting out the basic dimensions of the four temperaments, a far simpler matrix approach introduced by Keirsey in *Please Understand Me II*.

In essence, Keirsey holds that the four temperaments are the underlying patterns of personality because they reflect the two most fundamental parts of life—what we *Say* and what we *Do*.

First, people can't help but talk about what they're interested in, and Keirsey has observed that some people's conversations are primarily about external, down-to-earth, concrete things they can see, touch, steer, kick, cook, count, polish, and so on. While other people's words are primarily about internal, head-in-the-clouds, abstract ideas they create in their imagination and ponder at length: theories and speculations, dreams and experiments, philosophies and fantasies, and the like. Everyone does both at times, of course, but to put it in simple terms, some people talk mostly about *what is* and others talk mostly about *what's possible*.

Second, people naturally try to accomplish things, and Keirsey has noted that in going about their business some people think first of doing what is effective and gets results, and only then check to see if they're obeying the rules. Other people think first of doing the right thing, in keeping with accepted laws and rules, or with their own moral or ethical code, and only then concern themselves with how effective or productive their actions are. These can overlap, certainly, but again in simple terms some people instinctively do *what works*, while others instinctively do *what's right*.

Now, the combinations of Saying and Doing can best be sorted out in a four cell matrix:

Saying

	What Is	What's Possible
What Works	Say what is **Artisan** Do what works	Say what's possible **Rational** Do what works
What's Right	Say what is **Guardian** Do what's right	Say what's possible **Idealist** Do what's right

Doing

By looking at each cell, one at a time, we can get a good idea of the nature of the four temperaments. Thus, for the most part,

• **Artisans** speak of what they can see right in front of them and can get their hands on, and they're willing to do whatever gives them a quick, effective payoff, even if they have to bend the rules.

• **Guardians** speak of what they can keep an eye on and take good care of, and in getting things done they're careful to obey the laws, follow the rules, and respect the rights of others.

• **Idealists** speak of what they hope for and imagine *might* be, and they want to act in good conscience, always trying to reach their goals without compromising their personal code of ethics.

• **Rationals** speak of what they want to learn and plan to accomplish, and they act as efficiently as possible to achieve their objectives, brushing aside rules and conventions if need be.

So, want to get a quick read on the four temperaments and be able to spot them in other people? Keirsey's method is the easiest and most accurate I've found:

(1) Listen to what people **speak** about: concrete things and experiences (*what is*), or abstract ideas and imaginings (*what's possible*).

(2) Watch what people **do**: what gets results (*what works*), or what is the good or proper thing (*what's right*).

Learning to observe these patterns of behavior in people is the first step along the road to developing Foursight.

...Four Different Folks

As I mentioned at the outset, the four Hogwarts residence houses in the *Harry Potter* books match up amazingly well with the basic character of Keirsey's four temperaments.

• **Slytherin** is the house for students known as being "resourceful...with a certain disregard for rules," also "shrewd" and "cunning folk [who] use any means to achieve their ends." Sounds suspiciously like Keirsey's Artisans.

• **Hufflepuff** is home to students who are "hard workers," also "just and loyal,...patient...true, and unafraid of toil." Who but Keirsey's Guardians?

• **Gryffindor** welcomes those students known for their "chivalry," and who are willing to fight for what is "right and good." Very much like Keirsey's Idealists.

• **Ravenclaw** is the "wise old" house, reserved for only the "cleverest" students, those of "ready mind...wit and learning." Definitely Keirsey's Rationals.

Not that all students of the same temperament are sorted into the same house. J.K. Rowling clearly wants to establish four different kinds of personality in her stories, but she's careful not to segregate them rigidly. In fact, the four heroes in the first several books—four nearly inseparable friends—are all Gryffindors, and each represents one of the four temperaments:

• **Hagrid** is an impulsive **Artisan**, a gentle giant expelled in his 3rd year for disobeying the rules.

• **Ron Weasley** is a loyal **Guardian** whose secret ambition is to be Gryffindor house prefect like his older brother.

• **Harry** is a spirited **Idealist** who must fight the evil that destroyed his family, while trying to understand his own divided nature.

• **Hermione Granger** is a spunky little **Rational** who keeps her nose in her books and who knows all the answers.

From Hippocrates to Harry Potter, then, these four patterns of personality show up again and again, almost, Keirsey says, as if they're woven into the fabric of human nature.

* * * * *

The next chapter looks at the four temperaments in much more detail. Then come three chapters that explain how knowing something about temperament can help with dating and mating (Chapter 3), with raising children (Chapter 4), and with choosing the right career (Chapter 5). Finally, the sixteen personality type portraits (the four varieties of each temperament) can be found in the Appendix.

There are a number of ways of proceeding. Some readers might plow straight through, first page to last, while others will want to skip around at their pleasure. Some might skim for the essential ideas, while others will pore over every word.

But remember: we are all different, and we read books—as we do just about everything else—according to our temperament.

2

Portraits of Temperament

Once upon a time, in the land of Oz, four characters set out on a strange and difficult journey. Each was lacking something essential in life, and each wanted to find the mighty Wizard of Oz and ask him for his help.

• **The Lion** had lost his nerve, and he wanted Oz to give him back his courage. "As long as I know myself to be a coward I shall be unhappy," he said.

• **Dorothy** had lost her way home, and she wanted Oz to return her safely back to her Aunt and Uncle's farm. "There's no place like home," she said.

• **The Tin Woodman** was stiff with rust, and he wanted the Wizard to give him a warm, loving heart beating in his chest. "No one can love who has no heart," he sighed.

• **The Scarecrow**'s head was stuffed with straw, and he wanted Oz to give him a brain. "Brains are the only things worth having in this world," he said.

Courage, Security, Heart, and Brains: the four wishes of the *Wizard of Oz* characters reflect the nature of the four temperaments—the four very different patterns of personality that have been described in mankind over and over again, for more than two thousand years.

What Is Temperament?

But before we begin exploring the four temperaments, let's try to get clear what is this thing called "temperament."

In essence, temperament is an inherent personal style, a predisposition that forms the basis of all our natural inclinations: what we think and feel, what we want and need, what we say and do. In other words, temperament is the inborn, ingrained, factory-installed, God-given, hard-wired base of our personality.

In Keirsey's view, the signs of this underlying makeup can be observed from an early age (some features earlier than others) long before families, peer groups, or social forces have made their imprint on our character. This means that all of us, in the course of growing up—and unless seriously interfered with—will develop a consistent pattern of attitudes and actions that express our temperament.

A Brief History

The idea that human beings come in four basic patterns has been around a long time. A very long time. In ancient Greece, Plato and Aristotle each saw society as made up of four kinds of people playing four different roles in society, but it was Hippocrates, often called the "father" of western medicine, who first spoke of four mental or moral dispositions. Around 370 B.C. Hippocrates proposed that our temperament is determined by the balance of our four essential body fluids: if our blood dominates us we are "cheerful" in temperament; if our black bile, we are "somber" in temperament; if our yellow bile, we are "enthusiastic" in temperament; and if our phlegm, we are "calm" in temperament. While modern science has long since discarded this ancient physiology, the four fluids (later called "humours"), and their corresponding four temperaments, described patterns so universal in people that they became the foundation of Greek and Roman medicine and psychology. In fact, it was the Roman physician Galen (c. 190 A.D.) who gave the four temperaments the names they have been known by through the ages: "Sanguine," "Melancholic," "Choleric," and "Phlegmatic."

The observation of a four-part human nature dates back even further in Judeo-Christian writings. As early as 590 B.C. the Old Testament prophet Ezekiel beheld mankind as embodied in "four living creatures" each with "four faces"—that of a lion, that of an ox, that of a man, and that of an eagle—a vision repeated around 96 A.D. in The Revelation of St. John. Also the Church chose to have four Gospels in the New Testament, written by men of four temperaments: the spontaneous Mark, the historical Matthew, the spiritual

John, and the scholarly Luke. Irenaeus, Bishop of Lyon, explained (in 185 A.D.) why four Gospels were necessary: "Living Creatures are quadriform," he wrote, and so "the Gospel also is quadriform."

This notion of four basic temperaments, rooted in Greco-Roman medicine and in Biblical tradition, came to flower in the science and literature of Renaissance Europe. References to the four humours appear in the Chaucer's poetry, in Montaigne's essays, in Francis Bacon's and William Harvey's scientific writings, and throughout Shakespeare's plays. And Paracelsus, a 16th century Viennese physician, created his own temperament mythology, characterizing people with four totem spirits: changeable "Salamanders," industrious "Gnomes," inspiring "Nymphs," and curious "Sylphs."

As the Age of Reason took hold in 18th century Europe, philosophers such as Hume in Scotland, Voltaire and Rousseau in France, and Kant in Germany considered the four temperaments a matter of common knowledge. 19th century novelists, from Jane Austen and the Brontë sisters to George Eliot and Tolstoy, built characters on these four patterns of personality. And some early 20th century artists were also thinking along these lines. In 1901 the Danish composer Carl Nielsen subtitled his second symphony "The Four Temperaments," and in 1921 D.H. Lawrence wrote of human nature as being organized around "four poles of dynamic consciousness."

Even so, the ancient idea of mankind as a vital organism animated by four different spirits was all but killed off early in the 20th century, owing (Keirsey argues) to the powerful influence of Freud and Pavlov, whose work suggested that all people have basically the same drives. Temperament theory was barely kept alive by a handful of obscure behavioral scientists (Keirsey credits Eric Adickes, Eduard Spränger, and Ernst Kretschmer).

Then in the late 1950s, Isabel Myers came along and, building on Jung's theories, did the work on personality type that led to Keirsey writing *Please Understand Me*, the book that revived popular interest in the four temperaments—or as Keirsey called them in 1978, the artful Dionysians, the dutiful Epimetheans, the soulful Apollonians, and the technological Prometheans.

The table on the next page presents only a few of the highlights in the long history of the four temperaments. Scanning the lists, it is compelling to see just how consistent and true-to-type the observation of the four temperaments has been over the centuries. Surely this idea would not have been accepted for so long, by so many people, in so many countries, had there not been some sort of widely shared recognition of its validity.

Temperament: Traits, Characters, and Metafours

Ezekiel c590 B.C.	Lion (bold)	Ox (sturdy)	Man (humane)	Eagle (far-seeing)
Hippocrates c370	Cheerful	Somber	Enthusiastic	Calm
Plato c340	Artistic	Sensible	Intuitive	Reasoning
Artistotle c325	Sensual	Material	Ethical	Logical
Irenaeus 185 A.D.	Spontaneous	Historical	Spiritual	Scholarly
Galen c190	Sanguine	Melancholic	Choleric	Phlegmatic
Paracelsus c1550	Salamander (changeable)	Gnome (industrious)	Nymph (inspiring)	Sylph (curious)
Adickes 1905	Innovative	Traditional	Doctrinaire	Skeptical
Spränger 1914	Aesthetic	Economic	Religious	Theoretical
Kretschmer 1920	Manic	Depressive	Oversensitive	Insensitive
Myers 1958	Perceiving	Judging	Feeling	Thinking
Keirsey 1978	Dionysian (artful)	Epimethean (dutiful)	Apollonian (soulful)	Promethean (technological)
Keirsey 1998	**Artisans**	**Guardians**	**Idealists**	**Rationals**

Let's look now at summaries of Keirsey's portraits of the four temperaments, starting with the one he named the "Artisans" in *Please Understand Me II.*

Artisans

The great spider was lying asleep when the Lion found him. Its legs were long and its body covered with coarse black hair. It had a great mouth, with a row of sharp teeth a foot long; but its head was joined to the pudgy body by a neck as slender as a wasp's waist. This gave the Lion a hint of the best way to attack the creature, and as he knew it was easier to fight it asleep than awake, he gave a great spring and landed directly upon the monster's back. Then, with one blow of his heavy paw, all armed with sharp claws, he knocked the spider's head from its body. Jumping down, he watched it until the long legs stopped wiggling, when he knew it was quite dead.

The Lion went back...and said, proudly, "You need fear your enemy no longer."

Only a few Artisans have the opportunity to act this heroically in life, but they're all part of what might be called the *action* temperament. Artisans are born for action, particularly for artful action—in other words, for making free, spontaneous maneuvers that get quick, effective results. With what seems an instinctive ability to come up with just the right move at just the right time, Artisans have a natural talent for all the arts, not only the fine arts but also the dramatic, athletic, military, political, and financial arts. Think about it: who are the most famous painters, musicians, actors, athletes, politicians, warriors, deal-makers, and so on—all clearly persons of action in the moment—if not Artisans?

Artisans: at a glance

Artisans are most at home in the external world of solid objects that can be made and manipulated, and of real-life events that can be experienced in the here and now. Artisans have keen senses, and love working with their hands. They seem right at home with tools, instruments, and vehicles of all kinds, and their actions are usually aimed at getting them where they want to go, and as quickly as possible. Thus Artisans will strike off boldly down roads that others might consider risky or impossible, doing whatever it takes, rules or no rules, to accomplish their goals. Artisans have this same carefree, optimistic, full-speed-ahead way with people, and this makes them often irresistibly charming with family, friends, and co-workers.

Artisans want to be where the action is; they seek out adventure and hunger for pleasure and stimulation. They believe that variety is the spice of life, and that doing things that aren't fun or exciting is a waste of time. Artisans are impulsive, adaptable, competitive, daring, and believe the next throw of the dice will be the lucky one. They can also be generous to a fault, always ready to share with their friends from the bounty of life. Above all, Artisans want to be free to do what they wish, when they wish. They resist being tied or bound or confined or obligated; they would rather not wait, or save, or store, or live for tomorrow. In the Artisan view, today must be enjoyed, for tomorrow might never come.

Artisans: a longer look

- **Colorful** Artisan speech is filled with colorful, vivid descriptions of what they handle and observe in the world around them. No lofty contemplation for Artisans, no deep meaning or introspection. Leave to others the theories and abstract principles, the symbolism and flights of fantasy. Artisans talk about *what is*, often using lively words and current slang as they joke around, describe scenes, and talk about the details of their tools, their toys, and their experiences.

• **Effective** Artisans do whatever it takes—*whatever works*—to get the job done. Ways and means must be effective to interest them, immediately effective, otherwise who needs them? If some action doesn't advance them toward their goal, then why do it? Artisans don't worry too much about making mistakes, or bending rules, or stepping on people's toes. They simply give some action a try, put it to the test. If it's effective they keep it; if it's not they set it aside without a second thought and try something else.

• **Tactical** "Tactics" is the art of making the right moves to better your position, right here, right now—and Artisans are born tacticians. Whether they're promoting enterprises or working with tools, performing for an audience or composing works of art, Artisans are always scanning for opportunities, always looking for an edge or an angle, anything that can help them come up with the winning stroke or the shrewd maneuver.

• **Physical** Artisans like to get physical in their work, using their hands & feet and their senses to operate almost any kind of equipment: machinery, weapons, tools, and instruments, from jet fighters to power saws, from paint brushes to ice skates, from scalpels to hunting rifles, from computers to electric guitars. Operating all of this equipment is a turn-on for Artisans, extending their powers and amplifying their impact, and those who give the time needed to develop their skills often go on to become virtuosos in their field.

• **Playful** Artisans are always looking to enjoy themselves. With their friends they have a playful, fun-loving, "let the good times roll" outlook: games are to be played, food eaten, wine drunk, and money spent—all just for the fun of it. But even at work they'll try to find some fun and turn their job into play if they can, losing interest pretty quickly in any activity that gets too serious. Life's too short, they say, so best to get your kicks while you can.

• **Optimistic** Artisans are the supreme optimists, facing the future with a positive expectation that things are going to turn their way. Even when times are tough, they're sure that their luck is bound to change, that things are about to look up, that the next roll of the dice will come up sevens. And once they catch a break and get on a roll, they're sure their luck will hold—and they'll push it to the limit. This incorrigible optimism also feeds their self-confidence. No matter how bad it's going, Artisans believe they can handle the situation, that they can pull something off, rise to the occasion, find a way to turn things around.

• **It's the Breaks** We all have times when we must cope with loss and serious setbacks, and Artisans look upon such troubles in an unsentimental, even cynical manner. For Artisans, life is chancy, risky, a leap in the dark, a crapshoot. There are no grand designs or comforting illusions to cushion the blows. When fortune smiles on them they ride the streak, and when their luck turns sour they simply shrug their shoulders, kissing off adversity with an attitude of "it's the breaks," or "that's the way the ball bounces."

• **Today** Artisans live for today with an immediacy that others can rarely match. To an Artisan, yesterday is water under the bridge, so forget it. Tomorrow is a long way off, so don't waste time planning for it. But today? This is Artisan time, which is why they're so eager to seize the day and make the most of it, to strike while the iron is hot and get while the getting's good. This is also why they're often so contemporary in their tastes, right in step with the latest fashions in clothes, music, food, etc., even setting trends in these areas.

• **Centers** Artisans want to be at the center of things, in the middle of what's going on, where the action is—"where it's at," as the saying goes. Not content to sit in the stands, or even on the sidelines, they want to be in the game, preferably handling the ball, their senses fully engaged in the action, and their performance vital to winning or losing.

• **Graceful** Artisans are proud of themselves when they're graceful in action, that is, when they're able to perform artistically, fluidly, and expertly in whatever art form they've chosen to pursue. Artisans will spend all their time and energy practicing their technique, styling and restyling their performance, pushing their artistry to its limits until they can act with effortless freedom

• **Daring** The Artisans' self-respect depends upon their ability to act fearlessly, with boldness and daring, proving to themselves, and to others, that they can look danger in the eye and defeat it with nerves of steel. This makes Artisans the world's great daredevils and adventurers, willing to take huge risks in order to show their courage. In fact, Artisans often find risk-taking so addictive that they try it again and again, pushing the limits and getting closer and closer to the edge of disaster.

• **Adaptable** Artisans have the ability to adapt quickly and flexibly to sudden changes, shaping their behavior in the moment, in order to make the most of an opportunity, or at the very least to land on their feet. This adaptability is why Artisans work so well in a crisis: they're always open to change, ready to roll with the punches and bend with the wind, and thus they're able to overcome obstacles that might stop others dead in their tracks.

• **Excited** Artisans are easily excited when they are children and show the same restless energy as they grow up. They love to be turned on, keyed up, pumped, wired, and can tolerate a lot of excitement for long periods of time—"never a dull moment" is their motto. Unlike the other temperaments, Artisans actually perform better the more excited they get, and they often carry out their most spectacular actions in the heat of excitement. They climb mountains for the high of it, they drive race cars for the thrill of speed and power, they bungee jump for the adrenaline rush.

• **Impulse** Artisans are impulsive, and wouldn't have it any other way. They enjoy feeling their impulses take hold of them, sudden urges welling up from within. They love acting on impulse, like setting off an explosion. And above all they trust their impulses. Don't think about it, they say, "just do it." In fact, to Artisans—the *action* temperament—a life of impulse, of action in the moment, is life at its freest and most spontaneous, no matter how dangerous the activity.

• **Impact** Artisans want to make an impact on people, want to be felt as a strong presence, want to make something happen, maybe by closing the big deal or scoring the winning touchdown, but even, if need be, by defying or shocking the establishment. Artisans are almost hungry to do something striking, to make their mark, whether in the world of art or corporate business, on the battlefield or ball field, on stage or in the political arena.

• **Generous** Artisans have a truly generous nature. They see the world as a place of bounty and plenty—the glass is always half full—and they never really lose the pleasure that comes with free, spontaneous, "what's mine is yours" generosity. Even if they don't have much themselves, they'll give the shirt off their back, and just because they feel like it, to anyone who's down on their luck.

Artisans: in the movies

To help bring this word portrait alive, here are a dozen unforgettable Artisan characters in the movies:

- Muhammad Ali (Will Smith) in *Ali*
- James Bond (Sean Connery) in *Goldfinger* etc.
- Fanny Brice (Barbra Streisand) in *Funny Girl*
- Erin Brockovich (Julia Roberts) in *Erin Brockovich*
- Harry Callahan (Clint Eastwood) in *Dirty Harry*
- Jack Dawson (Leonardo DiCaprio) in *Titanic*
- Pete "Maverick" Mitchell (Tom Cruise) in *Top Gun*
- Shirley Muldowney (Bonnie Bedelia) in *Heart Like a Wheel*
- Alexandra Owens (Jennifer Beals) in *Flashdance*
- Hawkeye Pierce (Donald Sutherland) in *M*A*S*H*
- Satine (Nicole Kidman) in *Moulin Rouge!*
- Oskar Schindler (Liam Neeson) in *Schindler's List*

Since Artisans dominate popular films, and also have such a high profile in entertainment, sports, and politics, they can seem to be more numerous than they really are. Still, there are a good many Artisans, making up something like 30 to 35% of the general population. And, in truth, we are lucky for such large numbers, because Artisans create much of the beauty, grace, fun, and excitement the rest of us enjoy in life.

Guardians

Dorothy washed herself carefully, dressed herself in the clean gingham, and tied her pink sunbonnet on her head. She took a little basket and filled it with bread from the cupboard, laying a white cloth over the top. Then she saw lying on the table the silver shoes that had belonged to the Witch of the East. She took off her old leather shoes and tried on the silver ones, which fitted her as if they had been made for her. Finally, she picked up her basket. "Come along, Toto," she said, "we will go to the Emerald City."

She closed the door, locked it, and put the key carefully in the pocket of her dress. And so, with Toto trotting along soberly behind her, she started on her journey.

Home and family are the foundation of Guardian life, and they undertake journeys and adventures cautiously, and always with careful preparation. In fact, Guardians might be thought of as the *cornerstone* temperament, for they are the solid citizens given to establishing and upholding society's most important institutions: not only homes and families, but schools, churches, hospitals, businesses, neighborhoods, and communities.

Guardians: at a glance

Guardians are sensible, down-to-earth people who are the backbone of institutions and the true stabilizers of society. They believe in following the rules and cooperating with authorities; in fact, they are not at all comfortable winging it or rocking the boat. Working steadily within the system is the Guardian way, for they believe that in the long run loyalty, discipline, and teamwork get the job done right. Guardians have a natural talent for working with goods and services, products and supplies. They are careful about schedules and have a sharp eye for overruns and shortages. And they are cautious about change, even though they know that change can be healthy. Better to go slowly, they say, and look before you leap.

Guardians are probably the most social of the four temperaments, and have a lot of fun with their family and friends. At the same time they are serious about their duties and responsibilities. Guardians take pride in being trustworthy and hard-working; if there's a job to be done, they can be counted on to put their shoulder to the wheel. Guardians also believe in law and order, and sometimes worry that respect for authority, even a fundamental sense of right and wrong, is being lost. Perhaps this is why Guardians honor customs and traditions so strongly—they are familiar patterns that help bring stability to our modern, fast-paced world.

Guardians: a longer look

• **Factual** Guardians speak for the most part about the facts and figures of everyday life, whatever they can keep an eye on, take stock of, and take to the bank. Guardians can enjoy discussions of ideas (particularly about politics, history, or law), but they are more often salt-of-the-earth folks who tend to use common words and old sayings to speak about *what is*—concrete things such as goods and prices, food and clothing, health and finances, home and family, names, dates, and times, news, sports, and weather.

• **Law-Abiding** In governing their actions, Guardians are very much on the side of doing *what's right*, and for them this means obeying the law, both the moral teachings of their faith and the rules and regulations of their community. Guardians believe that strong moral and legal codes are the foundation of our civilized society, and they do all they can to see that everyone respects the laws that safeguard us all.

• **Logistical** Guardians seem to have an innate talent in "logistics," which is the part of any business that deals with service and supply. Whether their job is supervising performance or inspecting products, providing services or protecting people and property, Guardians see to it that safety measures are in place, that equipment is serviced and ready to go, and that the right people get the right supplies in the right place at the right time.

• **Managerial** Whether at home or at work, Guardians show great skill in managing the business side of operations. Guardians really have no peers at handling all the details of scheduling, inventory, shipping and billing, purchasing, payroll, regulation compliance—all those things that keep a workplace running smoothly. And Guardians also do great work in managing the home, taking care of the shopping, budgeting, cleaning, cooking, repairs, yard work, bills, taxes, and on and on.

• **Stoical** Guardians tend to have a stoical outlook on life, which means they believe that to be successful you must work hard and do your job without complaint. Make the best of it, says the Guardian, and keep a stiff upper lip. Life is no picnic and you need to get to work and not whine about how tough things are.

• **Cautious** Guardians face the future with a good deal of caution, even a little worry. They know full well that our "best laid plans" do "oft go awry"—or in the words of Murphy's Law, "Whatever can go wrong, will go wrong." And so Guardians believe the only sensible attitude is to expect the worst. This might make them seem pessimistic, but the truth is they are only being realistic about accidents and setbacks.

• **It's God's Will** In their times of loss and suffering, Guardians tend to believe that events are out of their hands, that some things are controlled by a higher source—it's simply God's will. In other words, Guardians understand that they are a small part of a large plan, and they have no real choice but to resign themselves to their fate, accepting life's misfortunes humbly, bravely, and patiently.

• **Yesterday** Even though it might make them seem old-fashioned, Guardians are inclined to turn their thoughts to yesterday, to look fondly upon the well-loved traditions and time-honored customs of the "good old days." In a sense, Guardians are the historian of their society or their family, for the historian honors the past, values the lessons of history, and passes on the traditions. As Guardians like to say, "The old ways are the best ways."

• **Doorways** Guardians think of space in terms of security and control, and so naturally they assume the role of sentinel or gate-keeper, standing guard at the doorways of institutions, and keeping a watchful eye on people's comings and goings. Those with proper credentials, or who follow the right procedures, are allowed through, but the unauthorized or illegal are stopped and questioned.

• **Dependable** Guardians take pride when they are dependable and trustworthy in shouldering their responsibilities. "No matter what," they say, "you can count on me to fulfill my obligations and to honor my commitments." If there is a job to be done, a duty to perform, Guardians feel almost obligated to do their part—and so they often end up doing more than their fair share.

• **Helpful** Guardians are always on the lookout for ways to do good deeds and to help their fellow man. Natural Good Samaritans, they do a great part of community and church volunteer work, lending a hand with the Scouts or the Red Cross, candy striping at hospitals, and helping the needy by collecting and distributing food, blankets, toys, and so on.

• **Respectable** Guardians are shy about tooting their own horn, but being shown respect by others in their business, community, church, or family is a great source of confidence for them. Their office at work or their den at home often has a wall filled with tokens of respect such as plaques, certificates, and awards, alongside honors such as trophies, commendations, autographed pictures of politicians, and portraits of spouse, children, and grandchildren.

• **Concerned** Guardians are truly "concerned citizens." They are concerned about their homes, their jobs, their families, their neighborhoods. They are concerned about their health, their finances, about how they dress, and whether they're on time. They are concerned about big things, such as crime rates, school standards, public morality. And they are concerned about little things, such as doing the dishes, aphids on the roses, their gas mileage. Guardians have broad shoulders, however, and all the many concerns they carry rarely get them seriously down in the dumps.

• **Authority** Guardians put their trust in authority, showing great respect for officials, dignitaries, directors, commanders, magistrates, etc., and also taking the word of experts and specialists. The power vested in the titles and badges of those in authority makes an impression on Guardians, but they also have a high regard for the authority of age and experience. At work, they give seniority its rights and privileges. And in their families, they believe in respecting their elders, as though age, by itself, confers a kind of authority.

• **Belonging** Guardians have a full social life, built largely around belonging to various groups. They are family people, and family time is often at the heart of their social life. But they also tend to develop groups of friends—a favorite "bunch" to have fun with, maybe a church group or a couples group, a lodge group or a bridge group. And Guardians also join a number of civic and professional groups: the PTA, the community service club, the political organization, the business association. It is vitally important for Guardians to be active members in any or all of these groups.

• **Steady** It's the nature of Guardians to be the stabilizing force in society, the rock-steady foundation of institutions—the Rock of Gibraltar. As the *cornerstone* temperament Guardians believe in keeping both feet on the ground, keeping things on an even keel, and keeping a level head. Guardians tend to be wary of change, conservative in their values, and careful with their money. They know all too well that getting wild and going too fast can spin you out of control. "Slow and steady wins the race," they say.

Guardians: in the movies

To help put some familiar faces to this word portrait, here are a dozen wonderful Guardian characters in well-known movies:

- Stanley Banks (Spencer Tracy) in *Father of the Bride*
- Loretta Castorini (Cher) in *Moonstruck*
- Hoke Colburn (Morgan Freeman) in *Driving Miss Daisy*
- Sam Gamgee (Sean Astin) in *The Lord of the Rings*
- Marge Gunderson (Frances McDormand) in *Fargo*
- Clark Kent (Christopher Reeve) in *Superman*
- Macon Leary (William Hurt) in *The Accidental Tourist*
- Lt. Colonel Hal Moore (Mel Gibson) in *We Were Soldiers*
- Eliot Ness (Kevin Costner) in *The Untouchables*
- Tevye (Topol) in *Fiddler on the Roof*
- Queen Victoria (Judy Dench) in *Mrs. Brown*
- Homer Wells (Tobey Maguire) in *The Cider House Rules*

In the movies, as in real life, Guardians aren't often the stars, but tend to take smaller roles, or even to be part of the crew working behind the scenes. Because of this we don't realize that Guardians are all around us, making up as much as 40 to 45% of the population, and usually doing all the thankless jobs that keep the world turning.

Idealists

Once the Tin Woodman stepped upon a beetle that was crawling along the road, and killed the poor little thing. This made him very unhappy, for he was always careful not to hurt any living creature; and as he walked along he wept several tears of sorrow and regret.

Thereafter he walked very carefully, with his eyes on the road, and when he saw a tiny ant toiling by he would step over it, so as not to harm it. The Tin Woodman...took great care never to be cruel or unkind to anything.

Idealists can and do get this upset about harming an insect, but they care even more deeply about being kind to their fellow men and helping them along life's journey. Idealists might even be thought of as the *personal growth* temperament, for they are passionate not only about becoming better human beings themselves, but also about nurturing personal development in their family members, in their friends, colleagues, students, parishioners, patients, clients—as well as in their communities, even in the world at large.

Idealists: at a glance

Idealists believe that friendly cooperation is the best way for people to achieve their goals. They dream of removing the walls of conflict and selfishness that divide people, and they have a unique talent for helping people settle their differences and work together. Such interpersonal harmony might be a romantic ideal, but then Idealists are incurable romantics who prefer to focus on what might be, rather than what is. The concrete, practical world is only a starting place for Idealists; they believe that life is filled with unknown possibilities and untapped potentials. And so they strive to discover who they are and how they can become their best possible selves, just as they inspire others to develop as individuals and to fulfill themselves. This notion of a mystical or spiritual dimension to life, the "not visible" or "not yet" known only through intuition or by a leap of faith, is far more important to Idealists than the world of physical or factual things.

Highly ethical in their actions, Idealists hold themselves to a strict standard of personal integrity. They must be true to themselves and to others, and they can be quite hard on themselves when they are dishonest, or when they are false or insincere. More often, however, Idealists are the very soul of kindness. Particularly in their closest relationships, Idealists are filled with love: they cherish a few warm, intimate friendships; they strive for a special closeness with their children; and in marriage they wish to find a "soulmate," someone with whom they can share their deepest feelings and their complex inner worlds.

Idealists: a longer look

• **Imaginative** Idealists live most of the time in an abstract world of imaginative ideas, spiritual beliefs, and personal insights. They see with their heart, listen to their inner voice, and most often speak of *what's possible*, what might be, or what can only be imagined: inspirations and fantasies, dreams and interpretations, myths and legends, symbols and metaphors, selves and souls.

• **Ethical** Idealists very much want to do *what's right*, but they base their sense of right and wrong more on a personal code of ethics than on community laws or social manners. This ethical code is often rooted in an Idealist's religious beliefs, but it can also develop from his or her reading in philosophy, theology, literature—or just from an innate sense of human decency. Wherever it springs from, it grows into a strong and ever-present conscience which influences all of the Idealist's actions and attitudes.

• **Diplomatic** "Diplomacy" is the ability to deal with people in a positive, sensitive way, and Idealists have worlds of talent in this regard. Easily upset by division and disagreement, Idealists look for what people have in common, for what they share, and they are gifted at helping people get along with each other—even care about each other—and thus work together in harmony. Whether teaching classes or counseling individuals, championing causes or healing conflicts, Idealists want to help people understand themselves and others, ever looking to enlighten people and to build relationships.

• **Personal** Of all the temperaments, Idealists have the best people skills. In business, they excel as directors of personnel or human resources development, those whose job it is to find quality people, to keep their morale high, and to help them develop over the course of their careers. But also working in schools, churches, social services, law, medicine, journalism, etc., Idealists care for others and show a willingness to become personally involved.

• **Humanitarian** Idealists believe in giving of themselves for the good of others, even if this calls for some sacrifice on their own part. They see all people as decent and worthy, and they will gladly donate their time and energy—and money, if they have it—to help their fellow human beings find a better life. This is why teaching and the ministry attract them, but also why humanitarian efforts call to them, as does missionary work, philanthropy, community volunteer work, and the Peace Corps.

• **Trustful** Idealists give their trust easily and wholeheartedly. They see good everywhere, and in everyone, and this makes them ready to take things on faith, and to believe what people tell them. Idealists might sometimes seem innocent, even naive, in their trustfulness, but they find it much more soul-satisfying to be positive and to put their faith in people than to be cynical or skeptical.

• **It's a Mystery** When facing life's tragedies, some Idealists believe that accidents are mystifying and impossible to account for—that reasons simply cannot be known. Other Idealists believe there has to be something more, some mysterious or spiritual force at work. The traditional religions—Christianity, Judaism, Buddhism, Islam, Hinduism—help explain the source of evil for many Idealists, but some will search for answers in the less traditional religions and metaphysical systems such as theosophy, astrology, parapsychology, dianetics, religious science, transcendentalism, spiritualism, etc.

• **Tomorrow** Idealists look to the future and believe in the promise of tomorrow. They see life as filled with hidden meanings calling out to be understood, and people as rich with unknown potentials waiting to be realized. With their eyes always turned to what might be, Idealists want to uncover these deeper meanings and to help others fulfill themselves.

• **Pathways** Idealists are most comfortable on the pathways that lead them toward the meaning of existence, or that take them on a journey to some higher stage of personal development. The whole notion of the spiritual odyssey, the crusade, the pilgrimage, or the quest is deeply satisfying to Idealists, and is perhaps their favorite way of talking about the place in life that means the most to them.

• **Empathic** Idealists have an extraordinary ability to empathize with other people, that is, they can identify easily with others, getting inside their skin and seeing with their eyes. Such powerful empathy is a source of pride for Idealists, because it's at the heart of their people skills. Their empathy gives them great and often sensitive insight into others, and it also helps them form close personal relationships—so close that consciousness itself seems to be shared.

• **Kindhearted** The most kindhearted of the temperaments, Idealists are filled with goodwill for their family and friends—for all of humanity, for that matter. Easily disturbed by hostility and cruelty in others, as well as by their own negative feelings, Idealists try to live in the spirit of friendliness and benevolence. To Idealists, in fact, feeling kindly toward people is a cardinal virtue, while feeling hateful or mean-spirited toward others is a sad human failing.

• **Authentic** To be authentic is to have integrity, to ring true, to really be the person you appear to be. Idealists need to feel true to themselves in this way, living a life that is genuine, free of façade, mask, or pretense. And if they sometimes catch themselves being phony or false or insincere—playing a role—they can feel deeply ashamed of themselves.

• **Enthusiastic** Idealists are highly emotional, quick to feel emotions and just as quick to express them. Fortunately, Idealists tend to be warm, loving people, so their emotional intensity is usually expressed as boundless enthusiasm. Particularly when discussing ideas, or sharing personal insights, their enthusiasm can be both delightful and contagious, bubbling over as they try to say it all, and often inspiring others in their groups.

• **Intuition** Idealists have a great sensitivity to first impressions, hints, suggestions, inklings, intimations, and symbols. They will follow their hunches and heed their feelings, trusting their intuition or "sixth sense" to tell them all they need to know. An Idealist's intuitive leaps can be uncannily accurate, and amazing to others.

• **Romance** One of the most important things to understand about Idealists is that, one and all, they are incurable romantics. In all areas of life, Idealists are concerned not so much with practical realities as with romantic ideals. But particularly when in love, Idealists have a keen appetite for romance—they are truly "in love with love"—and want their relationships to be deep and meaningful, filled with beauty and poetry.

• **Introspective** Idealists have an introspective nature, a pressing need to look inside themselves in order to discover their identity. "Who am I?" they ask, and "How can I become my true self?" Idealists are profoundly committed to this inward search for self-realization, seeking to get in touch with themselves and to become the person they were meant to be. This is, in fact, the basis of their idealism. Idealists—the *personal growth* temperament—aren't content with the person they are, or the world as it is. Surely there has to be something more perfect, more noble. If only they could find it....

Idealists: in the movies

To help flesh out this soulful temperament a bit, here are a dozen remarkable Idealist characters in great films:

- Frodo Baggins (Elijah Wood) in *The Lord of the Rings*
- Li Mu Bai (Yun-Fat Chow) in *Crouching Tiger, Hidden Dragon*
- Karen Blixen-Finecke (Meryl Streep) in *Out of Africa*
- Mohandas K. Gandhi (Ben Kingsley) in *Gandhi*
- Hamlet (Laurence Olivier, Mel Gibson, etc.) in *Hamlet*
- Viola de Lesseps (Gwyneth Paltrow) in *Shakespeare in Love*
- Sister Luke (Audrey Hepburn) in *The Nun's Story*
- Sarah Miles (Julianne Moore) in *The End of the Affair*
- Don Quixote (Peter O'Toole) in *Man of La Mancha*
- Jefferson Smith (James Stewart) in *Mr. Smith Goes to Washington*
- Private Witt (James Caviezel) in *The Thin Red Line*

Idealists are scarce, making up no more than 15% of the population. But the fervency of their ideals, as well as their ability to inspire people with their enthusiasm, has given them influence far beyond their numbers.

Rationals

They suddenly came upon a broad river, flowing swiftly just before them. On the other side of the water they could see the road of yellow brick running through a beautiful country, with green meadows dotted with bright flowers and all the road bordered with trees hanging full of delicious fruits.

"How shall we cross the river?" asked Dorothy.

"That is easily done," replied the Scarecrow. "The Tin Woodman must build a raft, so we can float to the other side."

"That is a first rate idea," said the Lion. "One would almost suspect you had brains in your head, instead of straw."

The idea of building a device—like a raft—to solve a problem and continue toward your goal is typical of Rationals, who might best be thought of as the *technology* temperament. Rationals instinctively look for technological ways and means of overcoming obstacles. They have a powerful desire to understand how things work, how to do things, and particularly how to build things. Rationals begin their search for technological know-how early on, as soon as they have language for questioning. And for the rest of their lives they continue to investigate the patterns of nature and society, almost driven to learn all they can about science and technology.

Rationals: at a glance

Whatever their field, Rationals set out to comprehend the natural world in all its complexity. Rationals want to learn about the abstract principles or natural laws that inform the world, but they are more interested in finding out about the structure and function of the world's complex systems, be they mechanical, organic, or social systems. And they are completely pragmatic about how they go about gaining knowledge. Rationals don't care about being politically correct. They want to find the most efficient or elegant solutions to problems, and they will listen to anyone who has something useful to teach them, while disregarding any authority or routine that wastes time and resources.

Rationals have a burning desire to achieve their goals and will work tirelessly, and with quiet determination, on any project they have set their mind to. They are rigorously logical and fiercely independent in their thinking—are indeed skeptical of all ideas, even their own—and they will try to clarify any discussion with their reason. Whether designing a skyscraper or an experiment, developing a theory or a business model, building an aircraft or an academic department, Rationals value competence, and they pride themselves on the ingenuity they bring to their work.

Rationals: a longer look

• **Theoretical** Rationals spend much of their time in an abstract realm of theories and conjectures—always brainstorming ideas and dreaming up new ways of configuring the world. Focused on ideas and concepts, on the visions and models they have in their head, Rationals tend to speak in technical terms, and often in deductive "if-then" sentences, about *what's possible*: plans, strategies, innovations, hypotheses, inferences, probabilities, contingencies, and so on—whatever's involved in grappling with the many theoretical problems that fascinate them.

• **Efficient** Rationals consider doing what's useful or effective —*what works*—as more important than doing what's socially acceptable. But even more than effective, Rationals always try to be efficient in their actions. They look for what might be called "minimax" operations, those that bring about maximum results with minimum effort. Minimum effort, not because Rationals are lazy—far from it—but because wasted effort bothers them so much. Efficiency is always the issue with Rationals. They want to get the most output for the least input at all times, no matter what they do.

• **Strategic** Rationals are talented at envisioning long-range, well-defined goals, and then at devising detailed strategic plans to reach those goals. Some Rationals are especially good at strategic operations, either masterminding plans or marshalling people and resources. Other Rationals are more adept at strategic design, either making architectural blueprints and models of new technologies, or inventing and constructing working prototypes. Either way, Rationals look far ahead and all around, their target always in sight, and their strategies leaving nothing to chance.

• **Analytical** Rationals invariably take a critical, analytical look at whatever they're working on. It might be an experiment or an invention, an argument or a methodology, a sentence or a book, an ecosystem, a computer network, or a political campaign—no matter what, Rationals are driven to break the system down and identify the parts that are in error and that need to be improved. You might even say that Rationals are error-activated: when they find a flaw in any system under their analysis, they immediately (and sometimes obsessively) set about to redesign the system, hoping to make it work more efficiently.

• **Pragmatic** One of the most important things to know about Rationals is that they're pragmatic to the core. This means that, in working toward their goals, they're always looking at the relationship between means and ends, and always trying to anticipate the practical results of their actions. Before starting any job, Rationals make sure they get their objective clearly in mind; only then do they set about choosing or devising the most efficient means possible—tools, materials, and actions—to make sure they reach their goal.

• **Doubtful** As if born a Doubting Thomas, Rationals instinctively question whatever they're told, and cast a skeptical eye on everyone and everything they deal with. We must take nothing for granted, nothing on faith, says the Rational, since all human efforts, even their own, are likely to be shot through with error. Best therefore to take a long and doubtful look at everything of importance—all evidence and arguments, all proposals and procedures, all means and ends, all observations and conclusions.

• **It's Up to You** Rationals face loss or adversity with a powerful self-reliance. To Rationals, events aren't of themselves good or bad; events are just events, and it's up to you to decide how you regard them—and how you plan to respond. This attitude also shows in the Rational's deep sense of privacy. Even in the best of times Rationals feel alone in the universe, isolated in their thoughts and emotions, with others unable to know their minds and share their feelings. And so in the worst of times Rationals react quietly, privately, the strength of their emotions known only to themselves.

• **Time on Task** Rationals don't usually understand or experience time as a timeline—as a continuous flow of seconds, minutes, hours, on and on, day after day, year after year. For them, time comes in unique, discrete intervals that are defined by the particular task they're working on. In other words, for Rationals time is not marching on, is not a medium in which an event occurs, but is a period of time created by, and confined to, an event as it unfolds. This relative time focus goes a long way toward explaining why Rationals tend to lose track of clock time, and can be oblivious to schedules, time-tables, and calendars.

• **Intersections** Rationals think of a place not so much as an isolated point in space, but as located at a point where two lines cross—in other words, at the intersection of two coordinates. Look at any world atlas or globe and you'll see lines of latitude and longitude. Or look through the eyepiece of many optical instruments (such as a rifle scope) and you'll see fine crossing lines—crosshairs—fixing the target. Seeing space in this way is probably why Rationals seem so on-target in their thinking, and why they so often have a sure sense of direction, as if they carry a map around in their head.

• **Ingenious** Rationals pride themselves on their ingenuity in accomplishing whatever they set their minds to. It doesn't matter whether they're engineering machines or coordinating operations, Rationals want to be brilliant in anything they consider their area of competence. Even playing their favorite games or sports, Rationals expect continuous improvement—and they beat themselves up if they make too many errors. The ingenuity they bring to mastering any of these tasks is the measure of their self-esteem.

• **Determined** Rationals build their self-respect on having a strong-willed determination. Once they've given their word, they will not go back on it; once they've set their mind to a task, they will not be deterred from accomplishing it. And yet Rationals never take their will power for granted, no matter how strong it has proven itself in the past. In fact, their greatest fear is that their resolve might weaken, that their will power might falter, even fail. They know they cannot conquer and control many involuntary parts of life (speech, for example), but still, when under stress, Rationals will often summon their determination and try harder to make it happen.

• **Independent** As much as possible, Rationals think and act independently, autonomously—living by their own laws and seeing the world by their own lights. They resist any effort to impose rules or restraints on them, and they will question any regulation or convention that aims to control them. Nor will Rationals accept anyone else's ideas without first examining them for error. It doesn't matter whether the person is a widely accepted authority or not; title, reputation, position, and credentials do not matter. Ideas, like people, must stand on their own.

• **Calm** Rationals prefer to remain calm, cool, and collected, particularly in stressful situations, when things around them are out of their control. Now, about matters under their control, they can get quite tense, becoming as tight as a bowstring when they put their mind to solving a problem. Even when they do start to get emotional, however, Rationals will try not to show it, and thus they are often criticized as being cold and unfeeling. But in truth Rationals are closet romantics with feelings just as varied and strong as others, just held tightly in check.

• **Logic** The only thing Rationals trust completely is logic. Only logic, they say, is universal and timeless, only its laws are beyond dispute. Rationals will listen carefully to new ideas as long as they are logical—as long as they are reasonable, well-argued, or based on a rationale. But they have little patience with ideas that don't make sense, and they will not be swayed by any emotional appeal or irrational argument.

• **Achievement** Rationals have an intense desire for achievement, a gnawing hunger to accomplish great things, that presses them constantly to work harder. Rationals live through their work. For them, work is work and play is work. In fact, once involved in a project they can hardly limit their commitment of time and energy. Unfortunately, Rationals have such high standards of achievement that they can have trouble measuring up. They often believe that what they do is not good enough, and are frequently haunted by a sense of teetering on the edge of failure. So what do they do? They buckle down and try even harder.

• **Curious** Rationals have a curious, inquisitive nature. They're always looking into problems, always asking questions, always wanting to learn more about how the world works, and how to improve the structure and function of its many systems. Rationals are the *technology* temperament, don't forget, and from very early in life their active curiosity leads them not only to investigate more and more complex problems, but also to acquire new technologies and new skills for solving them. They seem almost driven to accumulate useful knowledge, and to work long hours everyday trying to answer the many questions that intrigue them.

Rationals: in the Movies

More interested in learning than in receiving public acclaim, Rationals rarely get much of the spotlight. So to help make them a little more visible, here are a dozen great film portraits of Rationals:

- Ellie Arroway (Jodie Foster) in *Contact*
- Seth Brundle (Jeff Goldblum) in *The Fly*
- Eleanor (Katherine Hepburn) in *The Lion in Winter*
- Gandalf (Ian McKellen) in *The Lord of the Rings*
- Ginger in *Chicken Run*
- Henry Higgins (Rex Harrison) in *My Fair Lady*
- Eddie Jessup (William Hurt) in *Altered States*
- Professor Kingsfield (John Houseman) in *The Paper Chase*
- Jo March (Winona Ryder) in *Little Women*
- Morpheus (Laurence Fishburne) in *The Matrix*
- Annie Sullivan (Anne Bancroft) in *The Miracle Worker*
- William Wallace (Mel Gibson) in *Braveheart*

Rationals are rare, both in real life and in the movies, comprising as little as 10% of the general population. But because of their hunger to unlock the secrets of nature, and their drive to develop new technologies, they have done far more than their share in building our world.

Four Comparison and Contrast

On the next page is a table with all the attitudes and characteristics of the four temperaments listed side by side for easy comparison and contrast:

	Artisan	Guardian	Idealist	Rational
Saying	Colorful	Factual	Imaginative	Theoretical
Doing	Effective	Law-Abiding	Ethical	Efficient
Talent	Tactical	Logistical	Diplomatic	Strategic
Skill	Physical	Managerial	Personal	Analytical
Outlook	Playful	Stoical	Humanitarian	Pragmatic
Expectation	Optimistic	Cautious	Trustful	Doubtful
Coping	It's the Breaks	It's God's Will	It's a Mystery	It's Up to You
Time	Today	Yesterday	Tomorrow	Time on Task
Place	Centers	Doorways	Pathways	Intersections
Pride	Graceful	Dependable	Empathic	Ingenious
Self-Respect	Daring	Helpful	Kindhearted	Determined
Confidence	Adaptable	Respectable	Authentic	Independent
Mood	Excited	Concerned	Enthusiastic	Calm
Trust	Impulse	Authority	Intuition	Logic
Desire	Impact	Belonging	Romance	Achievement
Nature	Generous	Steady	Introspective	Curious

Oz Never Gave Nothin'

Although the four travellers in *The Wizard of Oz* wanted the Wizard to give them what they believed they were lacking—courage, security, heart, or brains—they were never really without these qualities, or as America put it in their 1974 song "Tin Man,"

> Oz never did give nothin' to the Tin Man, that he didn't,
> didn't already have.

In other words, the Lion was always a powerful, magnificent beast, and he showed his courage throughout the journey. Dorothy was never really lost at all, just asleep in Aunt Em's cornfield. The Tin Woodman was a tender and loving friend to even the smallest creatures along the way. And the Scarecrow time and again figured out ingenious ways to keep his companions moving toward their goal.

The point is that our temperament is always with us, and shows its stamp in everything we say and do, even if we have lost our way, or lost confidence in our personal style. Artisan, Guardian, Idealist, or Rational, we each live according to our own pattern, and we'll all get along better on the yellow brick road if we can begin to see these differences as strengths and not weaknesses.

3

Dating and Mating

For the last several years, four single, successful young women have been meeting each week in various restaurants and bars in New York City to talk over their love life. The four are great friends, and over lunch or cocktails they compare notes on their dates and prospects, on their turn-ons and turn-offs, and on their hopes and dreams. This is the premise of HBO television's Emmy-award winning series, *Sex and the City*, and while the show is stylish, sexy, and smartly written, an important part of its appeal almost certainly comes from the archetypal differences in the four main characters.

• **Samantha Jones** is a PR executive who specializes in throwing parties for clients, which is perfect since she herself is a fun-loving **Artisan** who's always ready to party. Uninhibited, sensual, and eager to try anything new, Samantha knows her way around New York City's night life, from the hottest clubs to the trendiest restaurants. Also no stranger to the bedroom suites of the rich and famous, she is not searching so much for Mr. Right as for Mr. Right Now.

• **Charlotte York** works in a modern art gallery but her own style is anything but avant garde. While surely no prude, Charlotte has a fairly old-fashioned, traditional attitude toward sex and the single girl. With a true **Guardian** sensibility, she longs for the security of marriage, wants children, and is looking for a man (preferably with a big stock portfolio) with whom she can settle down and build a home and family.

• **Carrie Bradshaw** is a journalist who writes a weekly newspaper column on modern sexuality and relationships. She is imaginative, introspective, emotionally vulnerable, and full of wonder about life and love. But most of all, and like any good **Idealist**, Carrie is an incurable romantic who goes from one special relationship to another,

44

all the time searching for her Prince Charming and her own happily ever after.

• **Miranda Hobbes** is a corporate attorney with a wide streak of skepticism and ambition—and also with a weakness for high tech gadgets. A **Rational** with a no-nonsense, pragmatic approach to relationships, she can seem tough-minded and cold at times. But Miranda is actually trying to balance her love life and her professional life, hoping to figure out some way to find a man worthy of her while still concentrating on her career.

Here again, and this time in a story for adults, the four temperaments seem to provide the patterns of personality in a quartet of characters. There is not one attitude toward dating and mating in *Sex and the City*, but four: Party Time, Home & Family, Romance, and Career.

Just My Type

Like the *Sex and the City* characters, most of us, when involved in dating, think about the men and women we meet as being, or not being, our "type." What do we mean? Probably that we are powerfully attracted to, and get along best with, a particular kind of person. It might be the "strong, silent type" or the "girl-next-door," the "nice guy" or the "party girl"—we've come up with lots of categories. Of course, other things influence us as well: physical appearance tops the list, but there's also social background, education, age, religion, mutual interests, and so on. And yet, as David Keirsey points out in *Please Understand Me II*, all other things being equal, temperament is almost always the deciding factor when we choose one person over another.

Since temperament plays such an important role in our love life, we might well ask what these patterns can tell us about our attraction to each other, and about our chances of living happily together. Are certain temperaments especially appealing to us? Are we more compatible with some temperaments than with others? In other words, when we become involved with an Artisan, Guardian, Idealist, or Rational, what exactly are we getting ourselves into?

Let's begin to answer these questions by looking at the basics of what Keirsey has to say about the dating and mating styles of the four temperaments.

Artisan Playmates

A number of things attract us to Artisans: their optimism, their spontaneity, their generosity, their physical grace, their playful sexuality, and many more. But surely the Artisans' most charming trait is the irrepressible sense of fun and excitement they bring to their relationships.

Dating an Artisan

Going out with an Artisan is a little like taking a ride on a roller coaster. Artisans live with **flair**, and will try to turn any occasion into a blowout **party** or a high speed **adventure**. Extraverted Artisans are often the life of the party, teasing and joking with everyone around them. But the more quiet and retiring Artisans are also full of **fun** and **mischief**, and seem to view dating as a **game** to be played or a wild ride to be taken. Never a dull moment if an Artisan can help it.

For Artisans, even more than for the rest of us, a good deal of the **excitement** of dating has to do with sexuality. Artisans enjoy talking about sex, joking about sex, and looking sexy. More than the other temperaments, they want to keep in **shape** and will work out at the gym, jog, dance, rollerblade, and so on, not just to be fit and healthy, but to turn heads. And **exploration** in sexual relations also has a special appeal for Artisans. As the bumper sticker says: "So many men...so little time."

In dating, as in all their other activities, Artisans want to try something **new** or take some sort of **risk**—just for the fun of it—and this means not getting tied down with one person for too long, but **playing** the field and experiencing as much **freedom** and **variety** as possible. Artisans are drawn to people **impetuously**, and seem happiest when pursuing new relationships, much as they might enjoy travelling in an exotic foreign country or driving a new sports car.

As dating turns into courtship, Artisans like to express their affection with expensive **gifts** and charming attentions, but also by promising to turn over a new leaf, to straighten up and fly right.

Artisans have the **chameleon's** ability to assume different colors, or different characters, in order to please the person they're with, and for a time they'll make the effort to become more like what's expected of them—more responsible for a Guardian, more soulful for an Idealist, more philosophical for a Rational. Artisans are quite sincere, and can be quite **convincing** in their makeover, although it usually turns out that the promised "new person" doesn't last very long.

Commitment is generally hard for Artisans; they prefer to **hang loose** and take one day at a time. When the topic of engagement or marriage rears its ugly head, Artisans will often remain silent and let their partner do all the talking. Or they will appear to go along with the plans, while actually biding their time, waiting for some painless **escape** to present itself. If pressured, however, Artisans will sometimes simply walk away from a relationship, asserting their freedom with few regrets.

Once an Artisan does decide to marry, **speed** is again of the essence. Long, drawn out courtships are not likely to hold their attention—"just do it," says the Artisan. When ready to settle down, Artisans may actually appear quite decisive in their choice of mates, but this is more likely the **whim** of the moment. Under the marriage impulse, whoever happens to be there at the right time is good enough, even if known for only a short while. Always **optimistic** and **daring**, Artisans are not usually on the lookout for potential dangers in relationships, and this can get them into trouble.

When it comes time for the wedding, Artisans don't care much for traditional, formal religious ceremonies, and would just as soon **run off** and have a quick wedding in Las Vegas. Artisans will put up with an elaborate church wedding for their mate's sake, and outgoing Artisans might even enjoy being the **center** of attention at a big wedding, surrounded by the beautiful clothes and flowers and photographers—all topped off with a killer reception.

But Artisans are often happier with **unorthodox** ceremonies, the kind that make a statement about their love of **action** and adventure: being married by a ship's captain at sea, being married while sky diving, scuba diving, bungee jumping, or the like. Similarly, the Artisan's idea of a honeymoon is likely to be **exotic**, and **athletic**: two weeks surfing in Hawaii, skiing in Aspen, sailing in the Caribbean, or gambling and seeing shows in Atlantic City.

Living with an Artisan

Living with an Artisan is nothing if not **exciting**; they truly do rush in where angels fear to tread. For Artisans, time, money, and energy must be used—right away—to try out the chic restaurant, the latest fashion, the newest nightclub, the hottest new car or motorcycle, without much thought for the cost. New **experiences** or new **toys** might well fascinate an Artisan for weeks, until an even newer interest comes along. And certainly in the bedroom Artisans prefer a good deal of **novelty** and experimentation; too much of the "same old" can start them wondering how to **spice** up their sex life.

For Artisans, money is to be spent and enjoyed, not saved for a rainy day. They might make a bundle one day, then **spend** it the next—here today, gone tomorrow—and their mates must be prepared to accept a life of feast or famine. Artisans mean no harm, mind you. They live so thoroughly in the **present** that they are sometimes simply unable to meet the financial obligations of marriage.

Artisan **impulsiveness** extends to people as well. Gregarious Artisans take up with people suddenly, easily, and have a knack for making **friends** wherever they go. Particularly at parties, these Artisans like to cut up with people, and they love to **tease** and **joke** with the other guests—just to stir things up and have some fun. But even introverted Artisans are known to collect buddies and sidekicks, and to spend a good amount of time and money on them, sometimes more than their spouses are happy about.

With friends or mates, most Artisans simply can't resist the grand gesture or the **extravagant** act. They love to give **gifts**, expensive gifts, especially if they have an audience. They will buy a round of drinks at the bar, or pick up the check at a dinner party, even if they're short on money for groceries. In the same way, a mink coat for the wife could well appear for her birthday, even though she might have only a few other clothes in the closet. The fun and excitement involved are what count for the Artisans—the **pleasure** of being seen as a **Big Spender**.

Married Artisans tend to satisfy their hunger for action through a number of **physical** activities. Artisan men spend a lot of time in their garage, working on cars or boats, woodworking, and tinkering with **tools** of all kinds. Also, they are often heavily involved in **sports**, particularly time-consuming sports that need a lot of gear (fishing, hunting, off-roading, surfing, sailing, skiing, and the like). At times their wives can come to feel like sports widows.

Artisan women love sports too (tennis, golf, skating), but they're also big on **arts** and **crafts**. They might get excited about gourmet cooking for a time, and then move on to try their hand at weaving or ceramics. Carpet, wallpaper, furniture, etc. are likely to be **colorful** and **unconventional**, and Artisans love to accent rooms with plants and artwork. Clutter is acceptable to the Artisan woman, and her home is often filled with projects in various stages of completion. Still, friends are sure to be **welcome** almost any time, and she will cheerfully push aside her projects to make sitting room.

Generally speaking, Artisans have **amiable** dispositions, and take their marriages in stride, not looking for a match made in heaven, willing in fact to put up with a great deal. They can have a temper, it is true, and may be quick to **anger**; but once they blow off a little steam they're fine. More typically, Artisans have an **easygoing**, live-and-let-live attitude, and their **tolerance** for nagging is remark-able—like water off a duck's back—although a carping spouse will usually find the Artisan spending less and less time at home.

All in all, Artisans make charming mates; they're entertaining, physically talented, sexually stimulating, and relatively easy to get along with. But make no mistake: Artisans need a long leash. Spouses must not begrudge them their tools, their toys, and their adventures, but provide them with a stable, tolerant home. Spouses must not deny them their grand gestures and their audience, but step back and give them center stage. And spouses must not demand too much responsibility from them, but appreciate them as the exciting, spontaneous, incomparable playmates they are. In short, spouses must learn to hold their breath and enjoy the fast ride.

Film Portrait: Rhett Butler (Clark Gable) in *Gone with the Wind*

Guardian Helpmates

If there is one temperament that best fulfills the traditional mating role, it is the Guardians. Loyal, dependable, hard-working, given to building a home and raising a family, Guardians provide a solid foundation for all our social institutions, including the institution of marriage.

Dating a Guardian

Guardians are the most **social** of the four temperaments, but in a pretty **conservative** way. Less interested than Artisans in fast times and night club entertainment, Guardians enjoy going out to movies, to club, church, or school dances, to amusement parks, ball parks, zoos, exhibits, as well as to popular restaurants and hit shows, not only to have fun, but also to take part in social activities and to **support** their communities. The more extraverted Guardians love to go to parties, not to get crazy, mind you, but to socialize with their friends and colleagues, or to take part in **civic** events, such as political dinners, charity balls, and VIP receptions. And though always **cautious** about spending a lot of money, Guardians love to go once in a while to an expensive place, a famous hotel dining room, for example, where they can feel treated like **royalty**.

On even the most casual dates Guardians like to observe good **manners**. The Guardian woman is charmed if she's met with flowers or candy, if the car door is opened for her, or if she's helped on with her coat. In the same way, the Guardian man tries to behave like a **gentleman**, and will show his date an **old-fashioned** courtesy, standing when she enters the room, for instance, and escorting her to her door at the end of the evening. Guardian men also take it upon themselves to make all the social **arrangements**, calling for dinner reservations, buying tickets, and so on. On their side, Guardian women like a man to be punctual, but they themselves have the habit of fussing over last minute details of dress or makeup, and often keep their dates waiting.

Observing the **proprieties** also applies to premarital sex. Of course, Guardians have as much curiosity as the next person—they're rarely prudes. But they are never casual or irresponsible about sex, and they don't usually sleep around. Even in an age of sexual freedom, most Guardian women have relatively limited sexual experience before they marry. Guardians are warmly **affectionate** with steady boyfriends or girlfriends, but they can be reluctant about going too far. For Guardians, there is still the unexpressed attitude that "nice girls don't." If they do, it is likely they have bowed to peer pressure—starting to have sex because it was the thing to do. Guardian men have more opportunity, and more social **sanction**, to sow their wild oats, but they tend not to do so freely, feeling instead a sense of **responsibility** to their partner, and feeling dishonest, even shabby, if they take advantage of a young woman.

Not that they are always so straightlaced. When Guardian men hang out with other men—at conventions, on hunting trips, on the golf course, and so on—they can rival Artisans in telling a good dirty joke. And Guardian women, while often prim and proper in public, can have an **earthy** side in private with girlfriends, and can enjoy jokes and sexual gossip with a shake of the head and a teasing "aren't you awful." It is with members of the opposite sex that Guardians try to be on their best behavior.

Guardians are the most **marriage-minded** of all the temperaments. They will go out with many people, and keep quite a social calendar, but if truth be told they're dating in order to find a suitable mate. This doesn't mean they're in a hurry to tie the knot. Guardians want to keep both feet on the ground, to look before they leap, and so favor long engagements which allow them to be sure of what they're doing and to satisfy social **obligations**. Meeting families is important, as is the **ritual** of exchanging engagement rings. For Guardians these rings are a pledge of **trust**—a sacred value—that show their intentions are **serious**. It is a proud day for Guardians when they have a firm commitment to marriage on their finger.

And while it can be exhausting, making the wedding arrangements is also a joy for Guardians. Obtaining the license, publishing banns, registering for gifts, shopping for flowers and clothes, mailing invitations, ordering the cake for the reception: all these necessary, **customary** preparations for the wedding—and so many more—give full range to the Guardian's talent for managing social rituals.

Living with a Guardian

For most Guardians, **settling** down to married life is a welcome relief from the lightheartedness of courtship. After the **traditional** ceremony and the **sensible** honeymoon, Guardians will turn their attention to what they usually consider the serious business of marriage: establishing a **home** and **family**.

As Helpmates, Guardians are ready to roll up their sleeves and work side by side with their spouse to build a comfortable, **stable** home life. Guardians enjoy **domestic** activities, cooking, sewing, gardening, shopping, and so on. They are **careful** with their possessions, and like to clean up their house or their car, as well as care for other household items, furniture, tools, clothes, and the like. Guardians believe that goods of all kinds should be used up, worn out, and then not thrown away, but donated to **charity**. "Waste not, want not" is a motto they understand. Also careful with a dollar, Guardians are likely to keep accounts and to **budget** strictly, planning well for their retirement, even if it means some sacrifice in the present. Insurance policies, savings accounts, government bonds, and other **safe**, conservative investments are the choice for Guardians, who don't like to take chances with their money.

Guardians budget their time as well as their money, and so are happy to live according to **schedules** and familiar **routines**. Not comfortable just letting things happen, Guardians might eat dinner at the same hour every evening; they might play golf on the same course every Saturday morning; or they might visit the same vacation spot year after year, staying at the same hotel (hopefully in the same room), and looking forward to the same activities with the same friends in the same place.

Socializing plays a big role in Guardian married life. They enjoy entertaining in their home, having other couples over for dinner and a game of cards. They join **community** organizations, both social and charitable—the Chamber of Commerce, the Rotary Club, the League of Women Voters—and they lend a hand in many community activities, **volunteering** for the March of Dimes, working with the Scouts, coaching Little League. They also take part in school and church-related activities such as PTA fundraisers, Christmas bazaars, Fathers' Club pancake breakfasts, and so on.

But **family** is even more important to Guardians. They like to keep in touch with their relatives by having family get-togethers, especially on birthdays or anniversaries, and by chatting on the phone. They are interested in tracing the family tree, and they keep track of births and deaths, weddings and baptisms, knowing that all such family **milestones** become more important with each passing year. Guardians also prize family **possessions**, and take great satisfaction in looking after the family heirlooms and collections and photograph albums. And having **children** of their own—children who will bring joy and comfort, and who will continue the family line—is often a high priority for them.

Now, making babies is as much fun for Guardians as it is for any other temperament, though their style might be more conservative. While Artisans, for instance, might expect a good deal of novelty and adventure in the bedroom, Guardians are apt to establish their **habits** early in marriage and to observe them happily throughout their married life. The exotic and the spur-of-the-moment are only occasionally interesting to married Guardians, making it unlikely for them to experiment very much with sexual techniques or partners. Although certainly not blind to the charms of others, Guardians prefer sex with their **lawfully** wedded wife or husband, and they're most comfortable making love at an **accustomed** time and in an accustomed place, a regularity which becomes more and more pronounced as the years go by. In general, married Guardians regard sex less as a form of recreation than as means of procreation, and also as a time of closeness that can **comfort** them emotionally and physically, helping them to forget their troubles and relax.

All told, Guardians make faithful, steady, reliable mates, just as they are loyal and hard-working supporters of social institutions. In so many ways, Guardians make up the rock-solid foundation of our world—they are truly the pillars of their communities, as well as the cornerstone of their homes and families.

Film Portrait: Henry Wilcox (Anthony Hopkins) in *Howards End*

Idealist Soulmates

Idealists are looking for more than life partners in their mates; they want soul partners, persons with whom they can bond in some special way, sharing their complex inner lives and communicating about their feelings and their causes, their dreams and their inward search for themselves. Idealists firmly believe in such romantic unions—the "match made in heaven"—and they have trouble settling for anything less.

Dating an Idealist

When dating, Idealists do not usually choose to play the field very much, but prefer to go out with one person at a time and to explore the **potential** for developing a **special** relationship. If they go to a party, for instance, they will enjoy the group for a while, but then look for a quiet corner where they can talk with their date on a **deeper**, more **personal** level.

Although Idealists would usually rather talk with their dates than do things or go places, chatting about literal or factual things isn't what they have in mind. Idealists want to talk about **abstract** matters—ideas, insights, life philosophies, spiritual beliefs, dreams, goals, ideologies, social causes, etc.—topics that break through surfaces and connect people **heart-to-heart**. Idealists love to talk about what movies or novels mean to them. And they will talk enthusiastically about art, music, and poetry, particularly about what some work might **symbolize**. Idealists will become serious in a relationship only if they are able to share ideas with their partner in this **imaginative**, meaningful way.

Finding the **rare** person with whom they can share their **inner** world is difficult for Idealists, and they often vow not to date at all for periods of time rather than go through the stressful process. For Idealists, dating someone means more than physical fun or social experience; it is opening their heart and mind to the other person, in some cases baring their **soul**, and carries with it both a promise and an expectation of deep regard and **intimate** understanding. And because they are offering so much of themselves, and expecting so much in return, Idealists can be deeply hurt when rejected, or when they have to break off a relationship. The **heartache** of breaking up can be so bad for Idealists that at times they will avoid getting involved for fear of things not working out. Or, at the other extreme, they will remain in a relationship longer than they should just to put off the painful scene of saying good by.

With the right person, however, Idealists can be **carried away** with their feelings, and the relationship will become the center of their world. Idealists have a way of **dramatizing** life, and so are not afraid of using **romantic** poetry and music to express their feelings. They will also give their loved one gifts, selecting with great care something with special or symbolic **meaning**.

Idealist not only make these romantic gestures, but they also tend to **idealize** their loved one. Idealists often have a powerful though often vague inner-vision of what their perfect mate should be like—usually it's an Idealist like themselves—and in the early stages of a romance they tend to project this vision of **perfection** onto the person they're with. At this stage, Idealists are likely to be blind to flaws in the other person, and to believe they've found the true "love of their life."

Although Idealists hate to admit it, such romantic projection often happens when there is a strong sexual attraction. For all their spirituality, Idealists are **passionate**, highly sexual people. But the problem is that, with their rich **fantasy** lives, Idealists tend to see imagination and depth of character in their sexual partner whether it's there or not. They also tend to romanticize sex as soulful communion, as something more than simple physical pleasure. In other words, when under the spell of sexuality, Idealists create for themselves a **dream** lover, even though it's often only a reflection of their own personality.

Idealists who try to build lasting relationships on this **illusion** are sooner or later faced with a bitter reality check, as they inevitably catch sight of the imperfections—either physical or personal—of their loved one. Fortunately, after this moment of truth, sobered up from their sexual intoxication, Idealists regain their keen **insight** into people, and either let go of the relationship or find an even deeper and more **honest** connection.

Once they have fought through the illusions and the projections and found their true **soulmate**, most Idealists regard the social conventions of marriage as less important, and far less sacred, than their personal commitments. Idealists are likely to follow their innermost feelings and **convictions**, and so will consider themselves married when they're sure that deep **bonding** has taken place, and when private words of **devotion** have been spoken. For many Idealists the arrangements and formalities of weddings can seem a needless burden, when the mating of souls and the personal vows are the important things.

Of course, if it seems right to them, Idealists will go along quite happily with the wishes of mates (or of parents) for traditional wedding ceremonies, and they will find enormous **significance** and **sacredness** in the rituals. Some Idealists will even take a hand in creating **nontraditional** ceremonies, writing their own vows, for instance, and selecting special contemporary readings and music for the occasion.

Living with an Idealist

Idealists embark on the marriage journey with high spirits, and they quickly devote themselves to personalizing their home. Idealists are imaginative and **creative** around the house, surrounding themselves with a great variety of music and art, along with cherished personal items, family photographs, religious or **spiritual** images —and everywhere **books**, not only books of philosophy and poetry, but books on religion and mysticism, novels of all kinds, and often children's books. Idealists have a flair for artistic hobbies, especially those that enhance the home, such as interior decorating, gourmet cooking, gardening, playing a musical instrument (piano, guitar, recorder), and often they become quite accomplished in the activity. Idealists will also develop other healthy enthusiasms, nutrition, yoga, meditation, along with various kinds of **personal growth** therapies.

Idealists care a great deal about keeping the romance alive and well in their marriage, and they will arrange for a romantic weekend getaway, a special restaurant, or an evening at the symphony or the theater with their spouse. And Idealists want to be great **sexual** partners. Seeing themselves as a **lover** as well as a wife or husband is a major feature of their personality. But it's important for Idealists that sex is **instinctive**, not studied or learned from manuals. This attitude can flatten their learning curve, but they certainly make up in **enthusiasm** what they might lack in technique.

Idealists also have instinctive **social** skills, and friends usually feel welcomed and well-hosted in their homes. Extraverted Idealists often become involved (and hope to involve their spouse) in a variety of **cultural** and personal development programs, such as Great Books courses, drama groups, and film societies, and they will also join discussion groups, talking over vital social issues and current trends in education, psychology, religion, literature, and so on. Reserved Idealists keep more to themselves, and tend to make cave-like **private** spaces in their homes, where they read voraciously and contemplate the **mysteries** of life, although they will actively support the arts and humanities in their communities, attending concerts, plays, poetry readings, and other cultural events.

But the Idealists' greatest skill is building close, loving **relationships**, and they are likely to be an endless source of tenderness, support, and understanding for their husband or wife. Idealists have an exceptional ability to **empathize** or identify with others—to see the world through others' eyes—and this makes them highly sensitive to the moods and feelings of their spouse. Put another way, Idealists seem to have their antennae always alert to their mate's feelings, and they usually respond with **kindness** and unconditional **love**.

However, such empathy can cause problems. Idealist antennae are so wide-band that it's almost impossible for them not to pick up the **emotional** distress calls of other people. Especially if they work closely with others in personal development (teaching, counseling, pastoring, etc.), Idealists can become so wrapped up in the problems and progress of their students, clients, or parishioners that they can find their time and attention badly **divided**. Whoever is there and asking for help gets it, even though their loved one may be waiting dinner at home. Idealists sometimes have to learn how to disengage from people and leave their work at the office.

Although their powerful feelings can pull them this way and that, Idealists are still unmatched when it comes to creating successful and fulfilling marriages. Their personal warmth and insight, their spirit of cooperation, their skill at communicating, their desire for deep, intimate bonding with their spouse—all of these qualities make Idealists truly exceptional mates.

Film Portrait: Newland Archer (Daniel Day-Lewis) in *The Age of Innocence*

Rational Mindmates

As mates, Rationals are loyal, uncomplaining, warmly **sexual**, honest and above board in their communications, and not in the least possessive. But for all the satisfactions they bring to a marriage, Rationals are fairly difficult to get close to, and forming relationships with them usually takes a good deal of energy and patience.

Dating a Rational

Rationals do not care to give much attention to romance. Not only do they find dating rituals slightly absurd, they also have difficulty engaging in play, which makes going out usually something of a trial for them. While some Rationals will try to make fun of social rituals by clowning around, they tend, on the whole, to be pretty serious and **cerebral**. For most, **academic** interests seem to develop at a faster rate than social interests—they are often the math whizzes and science nerds in high school and college—and they tend to prefer their books and computers to football games and beer parties. Often **late-bloomers** socially and physically, Rationals remain even into young adulthood somewhat stiff and awkward around other people, and many show almost no interest in dating.

When Rationals do finally start to go out, they make sure to **think through** clearly what they want from, and how much they are willing to give to, a particular relationship. Rationals always try to know what they're doing and where they're going, and only when they've **mapped** out their course—only when their **coordinates** are clear—are they ready to embark on a relationship. If they intend a short-term involvement, perhaps only for sexual experience, they make a short-term **investment**, and they make sure the temporary nature is clearly understood. Should this not be agreeable, Rationals will shrug their shoulders and turn away, with few regrets.

But not many Rationals are satisfied for very long with a series of brief, shallow relationships, no matter how well they have defined their involvement. Rationals usually want to explore the **complexities** of a long-term relationship, which includes building a home and starting a family. As with dating, when Rationals decide they want to settle down and marry—or at least to make a permanent commitment—they proceed with a clear **objective** in mind: to find a person they admire.

Here we need to draw a distinction. Some Rationals (Fieldmarshals and Masterminds—see the Appendix) are **systematic** in this search for a mate; they will often have in mind a list of features they hope to find in a partner, and they will not be slow to discourage someone who doesn't fit the bill. Other Rationals (Inventors and Architects) can be **passive** about the search, seeing the whole courtship process as troubling, even annoying, and they are likely to settle down with the first person of quality who happens to show an interest in them—just to get the mating problem solved.

Both kinds of Rationals can make errors: the first can be naive about their requirements and make faulty lists; the second can find that quick solutions lead to lasting regrets. But unless their choice is a complete disaster, all Rationals will stand by their **commitment** and make every effort to see their relationship through. Rationals have **no illusions** about finding the perfect mate, and when they've committed to a person, they are unlikely to change their mind very easily, nor will they voice any disappointment or dissatisfaction, even if the relationship develops problems.

Once Rationals have given themselves to a mate, they feel **pledged** to the relationship, with or without a social sanction. Society's seal of approval—in the form of a church ceremony or marriage license—means little to Rationals, and they will put up with such rules and formalities only to please their family or their mate. What matters to the Rational is **individual** commitment, and this personal contract is given all their **loyalty**.

The same goes for their view of premarital sex. Rationals consider their sexual conduct carefully and adhere to a strict **personal code**, which may or may not conform to current social attitudes. In most cases, Rationals aren't at all reluctant to become sexual once they have committed to a relationship, although they usually regard sexual promiscuity with distaste. A few highly **private**, seriously committed relationships is the usual pattern of a Rational's premarital sex life, most likely because Rationals (like many Idealists) tend to develop intimate relationships pretty slowly.

Living with a Rational

After they have made their search and committed to their mate, Rationals feel free to pursue their varied interests. Their **career** or field of **study** is very important to them, and Rationals spend much of their time—even at home—absorbed in their **work**, puzzling over problems, principles, hypotheses, theories, technologies, research models, system designs, and the like. Acquiring **knowledge** and solving **problems** is a twenty-four hour occupation for Rationals, and this can make them seem **out of touch** with the real world, and oblivious to the routines of daily living. Rationals also have a unique ability to **concentrate** on their work, which can make them seem **abstract**, lost in thought, as if a million miles away even when sitting with their spouse in the living room. The Rational, it can sometimes seem to his or her mate, "doesn't know I'm alive."

The problem is not that Rationals are cold and distant people.

They know how sincerely interested they are in their mates, and what powerful **passions** surge within them. It's just that Rationals are by nature preoccupied with **learning**, and have to be reminded to get their nose out of their books, their technical journals, their computer files—to get out of their head—and join the family circle. When thus absorbed, Rationals simply don't notice concrete reality very well, and unfortunately this can include their spouse.

Some things, however, Rationals need no help noticing. **Property**, for instance, is a part of down-to-earth reality that commands their attention, and owning real estate is often of vital importance to them. Ordinarily Rationals aren't very interested in acquiring or possessing material goods, but land is a huge exception, and might well have to do with their need to insure their personal **freedom** and **autonomy**—the idea of a man's home being his castle. Owning **tools** is another joy for Rationals, who will think very little of the cost of buying the latest, most efficient design of any tool they happen to find useful, be it power saw, video camera, or computer. Rationals love to feel **capable**, as if they can handle any problem that might arise, and so they surround themselves with the best tools available.

But more than anything, Rationals love owning **books**—they are some of their most valuable tools. A Rational's home is likely to be well-lined, or more likely strewn, with books: with technical journals and dictionaries, with works of philosophy, history, biography, and the physical and social sciences; but also with books for recreation, especially historical novels, spy novels, mysteries, and science fiction/fantasy novels, as well as books of math **puzzles** and complex game **strategies** (chess, bridge, and the like).

With all these books around, it's not surprising that for Rationals, as for Idealists, sexuality has much to do with the **imagination**. In fact, the degree of sexual satisfaction for Rationals will often depend on their ability to share **ideas** with their mate. The Rational woman, in particular, will in most cases be fully satisfied only by a man who can challenge her **intellect** as well as arouse her body. Obviously, this greatly limits her choices.

Man or woman, Rationals take great pleasure in having lively **discussions** with their mates—on topics such as economics, politics, history, science, philosophy—either one on one or within a circle of friends. Rationals are often **witty** and devilish in these discussions, enjoying puns and **wordplay**, but they will also insist that logic be adhered to. Rationals seem to have eternal hope that one day they can prevail upon their mate to become more **logical**.

However, just as quick-witted debate can bring Rationals alive, relationships that are full of emotional infighting can aggravate and exhaust them. Rationals love to spar over ideas and **theories**, but conflict on a personal level—from big things, like raising children, to little things, like taking out the garbage—is something they find destructive. Most often, Rationals will not let themselves be hooked into the quarreling and bickering, but will **calmly** step back and observe their mate's curious, overwrought behavior, waiting for the anger to burn itself out.

But sometimes, if they detect even the slightest message to behave in a socially acceptable way, or to have a better attitude—if they catch a whiff of social or moral obligation—Rationals will balk and **refuse to cooperate**, not only on personal matters such as remembering an anniversary, or saying "I love you," but also on seemingly trivial things such as cleaning up the kitchen, dressing for a party, or helping bring in the groceries. Their refusal might take some form of silent, passive resistance, or an icy blast, but it is rare for a Rational to yield to social conventions without some protest.

One other point about **communication** in Rational relationships: Rationals are reluctant to speak of love to their spouse, who are often, and needlessly, hurt by the silence. It's not that Rationals don't feel love for their mate; they simply can't stand to waste time and words repeating what's clearly established. The **ever-efficient** Rationals believe that once they have chosen their mate and pledged their word in marriage, they have indicated their feelings—and nothing more need be said. All too often, however, this lack of emotional expressiveness seems due to a lack of emotion, and Rationals appear to be **remote** and uncaring.

Like us all, Rationals need to be appreciated for the many qualities they bring to a marriage, and not criticized for the qualities they lack. Because of their thirst for knowledge, their fiercely independent character, and their logical focus, Rationals become the natural targets of spouses who want them to be more playful, more law-abiding, or more emotionally expressive, that is, of spouses who want to reshape them into Playmates, Helpmates, or Soulmates. But if their spouses—of whatever temperament—could be satisfied with the qualities that attracted them in the first place, then Rationals could be embraced as the excellent mates they are.

Film Portrait: John Nash (Russell Crowe) in *A Beautiful Mind*

Made four Each Other

Keirsey says quite clearly in *Please Understand Me II* that there are no right or wrong relationships—that individual couples defy generalizations. Whatever the mix of Artisans, Guardians, Idealists, and Rationals, any two well-adjusted people can be attracted to each other and find ways of making their marriage work for them.

However, Keirsey also makes it clear that, based on his decades of watching and working with couples, there are strong mating patterns among the four temperaments. It appears that certain temperaments tend to be particularly attracted to certain other temperaments. And these same matchups seem to have the best chance of forming stable, satisfying relationships.

To help explain these patterns, we need to recall briefly Keirsey's method (introduced in Chapter 2) for recognizing people's temperament by noticing what they Say and what they Do. Artisans and Guardians, remember, tend to talk about concrete things—*what is*—while Idealists and Rationals most often talk about abstract ideas—*what's possible*. On the other hand, Artisans and Rationals prefer to do *what works* to get things done, while Guardians and Idealists try to do *what's right* and stay within the rules.

Now, the mix and match of these two dimensions of personality not only key the four temperament styles, they also have a lot to say about the patterns of our relationships.

Guardians and Artisans—Lady and the Tramp

Keirsey's research shows that by far the most frequent pairing is between Guardians and Artisans. Of course, these two temperaments make up around 75% of the population, so clearly they bump into each other a lot. But beyond sheer availability, what drives this attraction? How can the careful, sensible Guardians be drawn over and over again to the carefree, adventurous Artisans? In the classic Disney animated movie *Lady and the Tramp,* why do Lady and Tramp, an elegant, proper family dog, and a charming across-the-tracks rascal, fall so hard for each other?

The first answer is that there is a powerful force of compatibility at work in this matchup. Guardians and Artisans are alike in one fundamental way: they both live in the real world of facts and figures, of physical experiences and concrete things (tools, vehicles, houses, food, furniture, etc.). And so when they meet, Guardians and Artisans are instinctively comfortable with each other because they are in their natural element, communicating on the same wavelength. In other words, they are both speaking a language they understand, the down-to-earth, literal language of *what is.*

But that's only half the story. The other binding force in this "Odd Couple" relationship can be summed up in the old notion that "opposites attract." Artisans tend to do *what works* right now, with little thought to the rules or the consequences, while Guardians want to do *what's right,* following the rules and being responsible.

And no question, this difference is attractive. Artisans are often drawn to Guardians as their "better half," admiring their stability and uprightness, seeing them as a safe harbor where they can rest and recover from their adventures, and sometimes even regarding them as saviors who can help them straighten up and fly right. For their part, Guardians find in Artisans a source of fun and excitement, and they feel a welcome lightening of the weight of concern and responsibility they carry on their shoulders.

Looking long-term, these Guardian-Artisan differences often find a comfortable balance in marriage. For Guardians, the high-flying, fun-loving Artisan is both a child to take care of and, at times, a wonderful diversion from their own nose-to-the-grindstone existence. For Artisans, the concerned, ever-responsible Guardian is both a fixed center for their footloose way of life and a parental figure they can enjoy surprising and loosening up. In fact, it often takes the moral weight of Guardian expectations to get Artisans off their motorcycles (surfboards, skis, sailboats) long enough to build careers or to raise families, just as it takes the high jinx of Artisans to bring a smile to Guardian faces and help them bear up under their burdens.

Points of conflict are there, to be sure—between action and caution, between rebellion and duty, between spending and saving, between freedom and putting down roots. But as long as these differences are taken in stride, with tolerance and good humor on both sides, Guardian-Artisan marriages do wonderfully well over time.

Idealists and Rationals—Beauty and the Beast

The same pattern holds for Idealists and Rationals. These two temperaments have one essential and vital similarity: they share a keen interest in the abstract world of ideas (theories, interpretations, books, symbols, analyses, stories, etc.), and thus they both speak the language of *what's possible*. When they meet, Idealists and Rationals know immediately—and to their delight—that they've found a kindred spirit, someone with a similar love of ideas, a shared fascination with philosophy and fantasy, even with the same passion for words and books. It's only fitting that in Disney's wonderful animated version of *Beauty and the Beast* Belle and the Beast melt their hostility and fall in love while dancing in the Beast's magnificent library.

Again, however, this is only one side of the story. Idealists and Rationals might speak the same language, but they are opposite in the way they govern themselves and their relationships. Idealists try to do *what's right*, letting their conscience be their guide and wanting to help others, while Rationals insist on doing *what works* to get what they want, regardless of rules and regulations, even in defiance of social convention. Thus in *Beauty and the Beast*, Belle offers herself in exchange for her father, whereas the Beast holds her captive trying to lift the curse that has blighted his life.

And yet this difference seems in the end to fire their attraction. Idealists deeply admire the Rationals' proud independence and clarity of thought, two characteristics which give Rationals a strength of character—a firm grasp of who they are—that the tender, soul-searching Idealists would like to find for themselves. On their side, Rationals are delighted by the Idealists' emotional sparkle and their loving way with people, so different from their own calm objectivity.

In marriage, too, these forces work for compatibility over time. Idealists bring a human warmth and insight to this marriage that helps the analytical, self-controlled Rationals put aside their books and take time for a family and a personal life. In the same way, Rationals bring a pragmatism and focus to this marriage that helps the sometimes scattered Idealists settle down and achieve long-range goals. And yet the real basis of their success in marriage is their deeply satisfying mutual interest in ideas. Right from the start, Idealists and Rationals know they have found in each other someone with whom they can dream the world, see far distances with the mind's eye, and, like Beauty and the Beast, live happily ever after.

Idealist-Rational relationships do not always remain harmonious, unfortunately. Conflicts of emotional expressiveness vs self-control, of intuition vs logic, and of ethics vs pragmatics can prove challenging in even the best of these marriages. Still, so powerful is their shared focus on *what's possible* that Idealists and Rationals offer each other the best chance of success.

We Can Work It Out

Let me emphasize again that the various other temperament combinations can also make successful marriages, even though they might have to work at it a little harder than the two relationships described above. Here are some prominent strengths and weaknesses in the other matchups.

Artisan-Artisan

Strength: Two Artisans inhabit the same world of external, concrete reality, speaking the same language of physical things, of *what is*, and sharing a need and a knack for effective action, for *what works*. Also, Artisans married to Artisans have so many interests and activities in common—travel, sports, parties, shows, clothes, jewelry, and so on—that they make perfect playmates.

Weakness: Unfortunately, with both partners living and playing so hard—going so fast in the same direction—they can quickly exhaust each other and move on to new interests. This pattern of two Artisans lighting up the sky and then burning out and falling apart is a familiar one.

Artisan-Rational

Strength: Artisans and Rationals both think first of doing *what works*, which gives them valuable common ground in a relationship. Both temperaments are irreverent and unconventional, and both love using the right tools to get results, especially if this means thwarting bureaucrats and improving standard operating procedures. Rationals also enjoy the Artisans' playfulness, and admire their spontaneity and effortlessness in action. For their part, Artisans can be impressed by the Rationals' vast knowledge and strategic vision, and they often like to jolly the Rationals up a bit, trying to keep them from being so obsessive about their work.

Weakness: On the down side, the "just do it" Artisans can grow restless with the Rationals' endless preparation and planning. And Rationals can get just as impatient with the impulsive, unreflective Artisans, and wish for a spouse with whom they could discuss their ideas more seriously.

Guardian-Guardian

Strength: Two Guardians both live in the factual, material world of *what is*, with their feet firmly on the ground, and both see the world in moral terms, where Rights and Wrongs are important. In fact, they share so much in life—attitudes toward work, finances, schedules, authority, home and family, and so on—that they are not much troubled by predictability in their relationship. Being two peas in a pod sounds pretty comfortable to them.

Weakness: But this similarity also presents its problems. Two Guardians can step all over each other trying to run the house and do for each other, both insisting that their routine is the right one. And worse, the quick-to-judge attitude of one mate is met with the same attitude in the other. Imagine two baseball umpires trying to call each other's balls and strikes.

Guardian-Idealist

Strength: Guardians and Idealists both want to do *what's right* and are both supportive types, and so they share a moral outlook on life and a wish to help other people. Guardians admire the Idealists' spirituality, enthusiasm, and vivid imagination, while Idealists, with their head in the clouds, feel safe in Guardian hands, anchored by their straightforward values and knowledge of the world.

Weakness: Guardians can regard the Idealists' search for self-knowledge as flighty and self-indulgent, a mere putting on of airs.

And Guardians can be badly hurt and frustrated when asked by Idealists to become more deep and meaningful in their relationship, with no clue about how to proceed, and with their redoubled efforts to stabilize the marriage only making matters worse.

Idealist-Idealist

Strength: Two Idealists speak the same language of ideas and imaginings—*what's possible*—and they both see the world as an ethical place, where doing *what's right* is the noble part. They can find deep satisfaction in sharing each other's inner world and exploring each other's personal development, each helping the other along the road to self-realization.

Weakness: On the other hand, if the pair are too much alike in their ethical concerns, or pursue the same spiritual goals for too long, they can become narrowly devoted to the inner journey and tire themselves out along the way. In addition, two Idealists can create a wonderfully empathic bond for a time, but eventually they can begin to invade each other's psychic privacy. Constantly getting into each other's skin can result in getting on each other's nerves.

Idealist-Artisan

Strength: Idealists and Artisans, while exactly opposite in both Saying and Doing, can still have a lot of fun together. Idealists love the spontaneity of Artisans, the way they live so instinctively and artfully in the moment. Also the courage and generosity of Artisans can fire the romantic imagination of Idealists, who will then project onto Artisans their own image of the altruistic leader or soulful poet. Artisans, in turn, feel close to the enthusiasm and romanticism of Idealists, so much (at least on the surface) like their own excitability and sensuality.

Weakness: Artisan fun and games rarely keep Idealists satisfied for very long in a marriage. They usually want more than a playmate in life, and they will attempt to steer their *what is* Artisan mate into the deeper waters of *what's possible*, particularly toward an exploration of personal development. Unfortunately, Artisans have almost no interest in discussing their inner life or their spiritual growth. So when Idealists ask them about "self-realization," "higher consciousness," or "spiritual awakening," Artisans do not really understand what they're talking about, and can actually feel put down for being merely physical.

Rational-Rational

Strength: Two Rationals have no problem stimulating each other with new ideas and methods, since they both speak the *what's possible* language of theory and conjecture, and both are busy figuring out *what works* most efficiently to get what they want. Two Rationals are likely to be interested in each other's research and discoveries, in their ideas and methods, and when they find the time to come together they can have invigorating discussions, logical, critical, and competitive.

Weakness: This competition can get rough at times—Rationals will go for the jugular in the heat of debate. But the greater trouble in these marriages is just the opposite: absorbed in his or her own world, each forgets to notice the other, thus doubling the distance to be overcome in the relationship. Rationals married to Rationals need to learn how to get away from their work and meet each other on a personal level.

Rational-Guardian

Strength: Although diametric opposites, Rationals and Guardians can still build solid marriages. Above all, Guardian mates offer Rationals one invaluable gift: a stable, reliable center in the home. Wrapped up as they are in their ideas and speculations about *what's possible*, Rationals often lose touch with everyday family life, and they need a Guardian with an eye on *what is* to step in and run the household. Guardians also see to it that Rationals have a social life with family and friends. Rationals need to be reminded to relate to people, and Guardians love to help their mates remember their social obligations.

Weakness: If pushed too far, of course, Guardian reminders can begin to sound like nagging, and Rationals will bristle at being told to do *what's right*. But a more important problem is that most Guardians, no matter how intelligent in their own way, have little interest in the Rationals' abstract world of science, technology, and strategy. Rationals might not need a great deal of idea-sharing from their mates, particularly if they are able to discuss their work with their colleagues. A satisfying social life, family life, and sexual life might be enough for them. But Rationals married to Guardians can come to sense they're missing some vital connection.

The Pygmalion Project

I want to end this chapter with a summary of one of the greatest sources of conflict in *all* marriages, what Keirsey calls the "Pygmalion Project."

In Greek myth, a brilliant young sculptor named Pygmalion decides to carve a statue of his ideal woman, embodying every feminine grace and virtue. For months he labors with all his skill, fashioning the most exquisite statue ever conceived by man—a figure so perfect that Pygmalion falls passionately in love with his own creation. Soon, however, he is desperately unhappy, for the lifeless marble can't return the warmth of his love. He has indeed shaped his ideal woman, but the result is only his own frustration and despair.

It's an all too familiar story. We often fall in love with people quite different from ourselves—as we have seen, we find these differences appealing—and then, once married, we set about to transform them into our idea of what they should be. The marriage license, Keirsey likes to say, seems almost a sculptor's license, giving us the warrant to chisel away, trying to make our mates into more perfect images. Not that we want them to abandon their own nature entirely. We simply want them to be more like us, since we all assume that our particular way in life is the best for everybody.

What we fail to realize, however, is that our mates cannot take on our way as their own, not at least without violating their own personality. The Artisan who lives on impulse is simply not very interested in obeying Guardian authority, in fooling with Idealist introspection, or in following Rational logic. And so it is with all the temperaments. They might be able to try on other styles to please their mates—for a while—but they will never become a different person. A leopard cannot change its spots.

Although we can't succeed in transforming our mates into ourselves, we all seem to want to try, and this does great damage in our marriages. By chipping away on our spouse we say, in effect, "You are not good enough. I want you other than you are."

Yet consider the irony if we were actually successful in reshaping our loved ones. Attracted at least in part by their differences, can we be anything but dissatisfied by changing them into copies of ourselves? In other words, if we win the battle—and it is a battle—to shape up our mates, do we not actually lose a great deal of satisfaction in our relationships? Or is our desire to control our mates more satisfying than accepting them and loving them as they are?

All of the temperaments manage to take the part of Pygmalion:

• **Artisans** urge their mates to lighten up, to have some fun, and to take some chances.

• **Guardians** work on their mates to take their responsibilities more seriously, and to be more respectful of authority.

• **Idealists** try to teach their mates to be more soul-searching in their personal life and more sensitive to others.

• **Rationals** try to argue their mates into being more logical in their thinking and more efficient in their actions.

And so, if we assume that Pygmalion Projects are a natural part of every marriage, then our job must be to keep our manipulation as loving, sympathetic, and good-humored as possible. If we cannot—if we resort to bullying, or nagging, or exhorting, or intimidating—then we have to expect our mates to defend themselves, and what might be called the "battle of the temperaments" is joined, a conflict much more serious than the "battle of the sexes."

But what would happen, Keirsey asks, if we could recognize this need to shape up our mates, pause each time the opportunity arises, and hold our tongue? Then we might, just might, remember to appreciate what attracted us in the first place. Then, and to that extent, could different temperaments live happily ever after...maybe.

4

Parent and Child

Since Disneyland opened its gates in California in 1955, it has enchanted millions of children and their parents. Disneyland calls itself the "magic kingdom" and some of the magic must surely come from the park's basic four part layout.

• **Adventureland** is the largest area in the park, for really it includes Frontierland, New Orleans Square, and Critter Country. The theme here is the fun and excitement of exploring new lands and facing danger. There are jungle cruises and clipper ships, pirate dens and runaway trains, Indian canoes and haunted houses, riverboats, saloons, and shooting galleries. It's an **Artisan's** paradise.

• **Main Street, USA** is the entryway into Disneyland, and it greets visitors with a nostalgic look at the safe, settled, hometown spirit of middle America a century ago. Here you find horseless carriages, bandstand music, a turn-of-the-century police and fire station, tidy gift shops, a family restaurant and an old-fashioned ice cream parlor. **Guardians** feel right at home.

• **Fantasyland** is Disney's wonderful world of dreams and make-believe, of storybooks and fairy tales: Snow White, Cinderella, King Arthur, and many more, as well as all the familiar Disney cartoon characters in Toon Town. Catches the fancy and the "wish upon a star" spirit of the **Idealists**.

• **Tomorrowland** explores the brave new world of science and technology. Featured are star ships and monorails, interactive automobiles and high tech water shows, sci-fi roller-coasters and automated displays of futuristic technologies. Just the place for **Rationals**.

So if, as advertised, Disneyland is "the happiest place on earth," it might well be because it was designed to make all four temperaments happy. It's not just a theme park, but a four theme park: Adventure, Hometown, Fantasy, and Science & Technology.

Do You Know Where Your Children Are?

Walt Disney apparently understood that kids are not all alike—that, in fact, they live in four different worlds.

But, then, almost anyone who's been a parent knows that, right in the crib, children have a personality all their own: four familiar types are "active" babies, "good" babies, "cuddly" babies, and "calm" babies. And when these little ones begin to grow up, their personality patterns develop right along with them.

• **Artisan** children are cut out for impulsive action, and will be into everything as soon as they can crawl.

• **Guardian** children are naturally concerned and responsible, and are interested in doing what's expected of them.

• **Idealist** children quickly develop a rich fantasy life and an intuitive feeling for family relationships.

• **Rational** children are calm and curious little investigators and experimenters even before they enter school.

Actually, the Keirseyan dimensions of personality (Saying and Doing) are easier to spot in children than in adults—children are usually more open about their words and actions. Artisan and Guardian kids naturally talk about *what is*, their friends and their sports teams, their clothes and their hobbies, their tools and their toys. Idealist and Rational kids are different, more interested in *what's possible*, and so they love talking about ideas and feelings, and hearing and reading stories rich in fantasy and heroism.

As for Doing, Artisan and Rational kids instinctively want to do *what works* to get what they want, and will bristle when adults ask them to "be good" and to "behave themselves." Guardians and Idealists, on the other hand, are not at all comfortable questioning authority or testing limits, and they try to do *what's right*, which means respecting the rules and pleasing the adults around them.

Whichever way you look at it, kids are different, fundamentally different. And this means that parents must not think it's their job to step in and form their child's character, no matter how responsible this kind of parenting might seem.

Instead, parents need to learn to respect their child's temperament style, and to find ways of supporting and encouraging the strengths of that style. Good parenting means being able to answer the questions, "Where are my children coming from?" and "How can I help them along the path that suits them best?"

To help find the answers, let's first have a look at what Keirsey has to say about the four temperaments in children.

Artisans in Adventureland

Artisan children get **excited** more quickly and stay excited longer than other types of children. But if they're easily wound up, they're also easily bored, and so always seem on the lookout for some new **adventure**. As toddlers they want to roam where the **impulse** takes them—turn your head, and they're out of their play pen or backyard. And as they get a little older, Artisans keep their eyes peeled for something exciting to do, or for something that **tests** their mettle. Maybe this explains why Artisan kids go for wheeled toys in such a big way, and why they never really give them up, their childhood tricycles and scooters turning into dirt bikes and skateboards—and eventually cars—when they're teenagers. Wheels bring them the thrill of **speed** and adventure, of going somewhere fast.

Natural born **risk-takers**, Artisan children are the first to play with matches, the first to ride their bike with no hands, the first to jump into the pool. Acting with this kind of **boldness** is vital to young Artisans; in fact, the worst thing for them is to be seen as a scaredy cat (or cowardly lion). Needing to prove their **courage** to their friends, they'll try anything, take up every **dare**, and answer every taunt. Here the parents of Artisan children face a dilemma: too little restraint might lead to injury, too much restraint can damage their self-respect. Overall, it's better to encourage boldness in Artisan children, otherwise they can feel ashamed of themselves.

Besides, restraining Artisan kids can be a difficult and frustrating proposition. If parents say "no" to something their Artisan youngster does—climbing too high in the backyard tree, for example—then the child must do it again, to see if he or she can get away with it.

Of course, most children will **test the limits** at one time or another, and to a certain extent, but not with the persistency and **recklessness** of Artisans. Like colts in a corral, Artisan kids have to kick every rail in the fence to see if it will give way.

Artisan children just aren't very good about following rules, remembering schedules, and doing chores. They might have to be reminded to get up in the morning, to get to school on time, to do their homework, come to dinner, mow the lawn, take out the trash, and so on. And Artisans aren't that interested in having clean rooms or neat and tidy closets. Their rooms are likely to be a **jumble** of toys and dirty clothes, sports gear and video game cartridges, all in a rat's nest, but to these little Artisans, just as they want it. They're too busy having **fun** to want to take time to put their stuff away or to hang up their clothes—besides, "What's the big deal?"

Artisan children shine in **action**, and quickly take to arts and crafts, and to games and sports—they need **physical** movement and novelty, and they love **contests**. In any of these activities, Artisan children are likely to give their attention for hours on end, and then will move on to the next thing that grabs them. They can spend day after day **playing** a musical instrument, they can spend hours at computer **games**, they can shoot a basketball over and over—only to lose interest completely and go on to something else. Those who get hooked on one activity will **practice** endlessly, as if nothing else matters, and can go on to become very highly skilled.

This is usually quite a contrast to their performance in school. Artisan kids—particularly Artisan boys—are often the little hellions who are unable to sit still in class, who make noise, bother their classmates, and who forget, or refuse, to do their assignments. All too often this lack of concentration and cooperation gets them labelled as **"hyperactive"** or as having "attention deficit disorder." They are then prescribed drugs to settle them down. What a shame. Certainly Artisans can act up in class, but this is because most schools don't offer them what will hold their attention. They'll concentrate and work just fine in a **hands-on** classroom, learning how to use **tools** and instruments, and how to interact and **compete** with other kids.

Parents and teachers must not forget that Artisan kids are not very interested in hearing about the past or preparing for the future. They live in the **here** and **now**, and respond to **vividness** and **variety** of colors, sounds, shapes, and so on. Like puppies, Artisan children are **playful** and full of **energy**, looking to have fun every day and in everything they do. This day, this hour, this moment must be spent getting their kicks, even if it means causing a little trouble.

Classic Disney film portrait: Peter Pan

Guardians on Main Street

If Artisan children have more than their share of mischief and rebellion in them, Guardian children have no problem following the **rules**, and seem happy when pleasing the adults around them. Little Guardians have an innate **respect** for their elders—parents, teachers, coaches, den mothers, troop leaders, baby sitters—and want to do what they're "s'pposed to do." In fact, they're proud of themselves when they show adults that they can be **depended** on to do what's expected of them, that they are **trustworthy** and accountable.

In the home, Guardian children, even very young ones, are busy beavers. They like to be given specific **responsibilities**, such as setting the table, doing the dishes, mowing the lawn, sorting the wash, and so on. They pitch right in to help with these routine jobs, and they respond positively to parental praise, such as "You did that just the way I wanted," or "I know I can depend on you."

Also at school they follow **directions** well and **work hard** to do all of their assignments and to please their teachers. In kindergarten, for instance, little Guardians (nearly half the class) will sit quietly and wait for instructions, whereas little Artisans (most of the rest) are busy tussling or chatting or roaming around. And Guardian first graders are delighted when they get a gold star for **good behavior**, for never being tardy, say, or for doing their lessons neatly.

Guardian children like to follow well-established **routines** and **schedules**. Guardian infants do best with **regular** feeding times, bath times, and nap times. When school age, Guardian kids are happy getting up at the same time every morning, doing their homework every evening, and getting to bed on time. Basically, following a familiar routine gives Guardian children a feeling of **safety**, while constant changes can make them feel upset and insecure. More than the other temperaments, Guardian children need to know that what is so today will be so tomorrow.

For this reason, frequent family moves can be hard on Guardian kids. They do better when raised in the **same** neighborhood, school system, and community, and with close childhood friends. Contrast this with Artisans of similar age, who enjoy changes and surprises. For example, transferring to a new school at midyear might well perk up an Artisan child with new opportunities, while a Guardian youngster might worry about learning the rules and **fitting in**.

There's no place like **home** for little Guardians. They see home first as a place of **security**, and they don't usually roam too far away, preferring to play in their own yards, or at the houses of nearby friends. (They also tend to stick close to their homeroom at school.) In fact, when Guardian kids go on trips with friends or to summer camp, they are likely to feel **homesick** pretty quickly.

But home is also a place of **order** for Guardian children, particularly if they're lucky enough to have their own room. Here they can work on their school assignments and hobbies (Guardians love collecting stamps, coins, dolls, etc.) without having things messed up. **Neatness** counts for most Guardian kids, and they tend to keep their desks and closets tidy, and their clothes neatly put away.

And finally, home is the center of their early social life. The first social group for any of us is our family, and Guardian children take to **family** life like ducks to water. They like to be around their parents, they get along fine having many brothers and sisters, and they look forward to large family **gatherings** at the holidays, with aunts, uncles, grandparents, and cousins filling the house.

Of course, Guardian kids develop **social** life outside the home as well. They make **friends** easily and usually have a gang to play with. And often their social life revolves around helping others. Even as young as five, little Guardians can be seen doing good deeds. In school Guardian kids are natural born teacher's **helpers**, often becoming hall monitors, crossing guards, student aids, class officers, team managers, etc. And teenage Guardians often volunteer for community **service** projects and join organizations such as school clubs, church groups, and scout troops. The friendly boy or girl scout helping an elderly person across the street is a stereotype of Guardian children that happens to describe them well.

Classic Disney film portrait: Pinocchio

Idealists in Fantasyland

What immediately sets Idealist children apart is their vivid **imagination** and sense of **fantasy**. Starting very young, Idealists love being read **stories**: they'd much rather hear stories than play with toys, and they might want the same bedtime story read over and over, until they finally fall asleep. They will even **dream** up their own stories and tell them to parents and playmates. At times parents might wonder if little Idealists are fibbing about something when the truth is they're living happily in **make-believe**.

Idealist preschoolers are captivated by fairy tales, golden books, and nursery rhymes. Then in elementary school, they begin to read every kind of **fiction** they can lay their hands on: boy or girl detective stories, science fiction stories, sports stories, ghost stories, but especially sword and sorcery stories, with knights and their ladies, princes and princesses, dragons and wizards. Idealist children **identify** with the characters in these stories, and the effects can be so emotionally powerful that they can dream of taking off on **quests** of their own.

In fact, parents and teachers might want to keep an eye on the reading (and viewing) material of Idealist children, who can easily become upset by the disturbing imagery in stories with dragons, witches, ogres, and monsters—all of which can show up in nightmares. Parents should try to introduce their little Idealists to books, movies, and videos that have **happy endings**, with heroes winning and villains being vanquished or having a change of heart. Such "happily-ever-after" stories capture Idealist kids from the very start and never really let go of them.

Idealist children play with their toys as fantasy objects, weaving stories around them, and **creating** worlds for them to inhabit. They have a soft spot for toys to which they can attach a human **personality**—hand puppets, Raggedy Ann dolls, stuffed animals. To be sure, a teddy bear or a favorite doll can be unbelievably dear to Idealist children, and a lost toy friend is a real tragedy to them. Also, Idealists are more likely than the other types to have an **invisible** friend.

If their fantasy life is well developed, so is their **emotional** life. Even at an early age Idealists seem **fired** with powerful emotions, and are hardly able to keep from expressing their feelings. Idealist kids trust their **heart** to tell them about their feelings, and about the feelings of others. They can occasionally be **prickly**, frustrated when the world isn't as perfect as they imagine it. But most often they have an **enthusiasm** and openheartedness about them that is rooted deeply in their temperament.

Also, Idealist children are often almost **oversensitive** to the feelings of their parents, and the emotional climate in the home affects them deeply. When their parents are in **harmony**, Idealist youngsters feel at **peace** with themselves; however, if their parents quarrel a good deal, little Idealists are likely to become insecure and withdrawn. And if their parents spank them, Idealist children can be deeply hurt, and far more by the cruelty of the act than by the pain.

For their part, Idealist kids like to think well of everyone and everything, and they do all they can to make others happy. The line from the song in the old Coca-Cola commercial, "I'd like to teach the world to sing in perfect harmony," nicely sums up the young Idealists' belief that they can make the world a **better place**. To this end, they do a lot of **volunteer** work, becoming tutors for younger students, and joining programs to help the physically and mentally handicapped, and the elderly. And if need be, they take on the role of **peacemaker**, hoping to settle disputes among their friends and family members. Idealist children seem to have a gift for relating closely and **positively** with people. And they express themselves with a **personal** warmth that clearly communicates their sincere interest in understanding and helping others.

At the same time, Idealist children need to be recognized as **unique** individuals. In school, and sometimes even in their family, they can find themselves **out of step** with those around them, feeling that they are different, not like the other kids, without realizing what that difference is. This can sometimes make them feel **isolated** and **self-conscious**, but if handled properly Idealist youngsters can actually take some pride in feeling that they are one of a kind. What they need is for their parents and teachers to recognize their **uniqueness** and, without singling them out or playing favorites, to acknowledge their special **significance** as a valuable member of the family or the class. Idealist kids thrive on an abundance of personalized attention, and the messages they most need to hear are "You are special; I value you; you are important to me."

Classic Disney film portrait: Ariel in *The Little Mermaid*

Rationals in Tomorrowland

Rational children seem to be born wanting to **learn** how things work. They start their **investigations** as early as the age of two, exploring whatever they can get hold of to see what can be done with it. Let a Rational toddler stand in the driver's seat of a car, and watch as he or she tries out every button, lever, switch, and knob over and over again. If they trigger any sort of light or sound or movement, the little Rational can be entertained for quite a while, learning how to **control** these intriguing responses.

How things work: that's what fascinates Rational children, that's what they must figure out by **inquiry** and **experimentation**. These are the children who want to take things apart and put them back together again. These are the children who have to think before they act, and who are filled with **questions**: "Why does the sun come up here and not there?" "How do planes fly?" "Why can't I have dessert before my vegetables if I eat both?" "What would happen if I pushed all the numbers on the phone?" These questions aren't meant to annoy their parents, but are simply expressions of the Rational child's powerful **curiosity**.

Parents need to be patient with these questions, and try to give answers, but they must also allow their Rational children to investigate on their own. Toys and games that let them **make plans** and **solve problems** are just the thing: busy boards, for instance, and construction sets of all kinds (building blocks, Lincoln logs, Legos, and the like). As they get a bit older, Rational children want chemistry sets, electronics sets, and Erector sets, so they can experiment with different **structures** and **functions**. They make good use of a set of encyclopedias, they have a special fondness for flying machines (from kites to radio controlled airplanes), and they also play **strategic** games such as chess and Mastermind. And, of course, the video play station and the computer intrigue them. Rational children love to exercise their **ingenuity**, and are quietly proud of themselves when they have mastered any of these activities or **technologies**.

In many of these investigations and experiments, Rational children appear **calm** and self-contained. But the calm exterior conceals a desire for **achievement** that can make them pretty uptight. Once caught in the grip of accomplishing some goal, little Rationals can become **angry with themselves** when they make a stupid error. Because of this, parents and teachers are wise to give Rationals assignments they can succeed in, and never to criticize their failures. Rational youngsters are particularly vulnerable here: they are **self-doubting** to begin with, and for them to feel good about themselves they must feel **capable**. Too many errors or failures can undermine their self-esteem, and even cause them recurring nightmares.

Maybe this is why the Rational child's favorite stories are about **heroic** achievement. Like the Idealists, Rationals love all kinds of stories—science fiction, fantasy, tales of magic and sorcery, mysteries—but they can't get enough **stories** about the great exploits of heroic figures, such as goodguy gunslingers, triumphant warriors, successful explorers, brilliant scientists, and ingenious inventors. As they grow older their collection of heroes steadily increases, and are seldom forgotten.

Like their heroes, Rational children are strong little **individuals** from the word go. They want to **think for themselves**, to figure things out for themselves, and to do things their own way. They question authority and will go along with a parent or teacher only if their statements **make sense**. Admittedly, such an attitude can annoy parents and teachers, who are concerned how to get this little individualist to join in the family or class customs and routines.

Now, since many of these customs make no sense and have no **functional** purpose, they are bound to be questioned by Rational kids. Table manners, for instance, are totally arbitrary and so are puzzling to little Rationals. **Pragmatic** from the start, they might go along just to stay out of trouble, but it usually takes them longer to catch on to the proper, polite way of eating. Or take cleaning up their room. No matter how often they are reminded, Rational children are irregular about straightening up their things. Probably the most frequent condition of their room is one of apparent chaos, but with the Rational child knowing where each and every treasure is placed.

Classic Disney film portrait: Alice in *Alice in Wonderland*

All in the Family

So: the first job of parents is to recognize and support the temperaments of their children. But parents also need to have enough

Foursight to understand how their own temperament figures into the way they go about raising their kids.

The truth is that not all parent-child combinations are matches made in heaven. As with marriage partners, some temperament differences in parents and their children can cause difficulties. The goals that certain types of parents have for their children are fine for some kids but not for others, just as the forms of discipline that certain types of parents use will be effective with some children, but can actually cause problems with others.

And yet regardless of the temperament mix, good parent-child relations don't have to be so much the luck of the draw. In this part of family life, too, a little patience, tolerance, humor—and some basic knowledge about people patterns—can help us get along well with our kids, no matter what their personality.

Let's turn now to Keirsey's ideas on how the four types of parents go about handling their kids, and on the pros and cons of each temperament style with all four types of children.

Liberal Artisans

Artisans might be called liberal parents, since they are usually easygoing and indulgent with their children, more given to expanding boundaries than to setting firm limits. Carefree and impulsive by nature, Artisan parents give their children a lot of freedom to do what they want, when they want, and they provide them ample opportunities for fun and games and adventures. Artisans actually encourage their children to test the limits of their world, exploring things on their own and learning the hard way about the consequences of their actions. The good news is that this free-handed Artisan parenting style can be just the thing for some types of children, allowing them to spread their wings and take off confidently into the world. But the bad news is that it can give other kids more freedom than they can handle, and fewer limits than they need.

Discipline: Artisans don't like having to discipline their children, so they're very clever in handling them to keep them from getting too far out of line. When pushed, however, Artisan parents can get pretty tough. They tolerate no back talk, and when angry they don't hesitate to speak harshly to their kids and even to spank them. But tough is not strict, and Artisan parents actually like their youngsters to show some nerve and take some chances. They believe that too many controls on children will make them afraid to act, and fearfulness is something Artisan parents find hard to accept in their children.

Film Portrait: Vianne Rocher (Juliet Binoche) in *Chocolat*

Artisan Parent—Artisan Child

Strength: Because they are alike in both of Keirsey's basic dimensions—saying *what is* as well as doing *what works*—Artisan parents usually get along famously with their Artisan children. Artisan parents take pride in these kids' toughness and charm, their way with tools and animals, their craftiness and their gracefulness. Like chips off the old block, Artisan children are more than ready to grab their freedom and run with it. They need no encouragement to be bold and adventurous and to take up sports of all kinds. They need no urging to try their hand at music, dance, acting, and other arts and crafts. Nor do they need to be taught how to have fun and to be popular with their friends. All told, Artisan kids are often the apple of their Artisan parents' eye.

Weakness: On the down side, Artisan parents can be so taken with their Artisan children that they fail to give them sufficient limits, encouraging instead their natural impulsiveness and unruliness. As a result, these children might push too close to the edge and get into jams; or they might come to expect indulgence and leniency from adults, and so have trouble with authority.

Artisan Parent—Guardian Child

Strength: With both parent and child well situated in the world of *what is*, Artisan parents usually have little or no difficulty communicating with their Guardian kids. Also, Artisan boldness and *do what works* attitude means that they have no hesitation in helping these children to get into a wide variety of sports and crafts and activities, which can loosen them up and show them how to have some fun. With such an example, Guardian children can overcome their natural caution, and have a good chance to blossom both at home and at school.

Weakness: There is a danger that highly aggressive Artisan parents can be impatient with their Guardian children's carefulness and concern for doing *what's right*. If Artisan parents expect too much boldness and impetuosity from their little Guardians, they will only frighten and inhibit them, and teach them they're a failure. Fortunately, the other parent in this family is often a Guardian, which gives Guardian children the best of both worlds: one parent to have fun with, and one parent to please with their good behavior.

Artisan Parent—Idealist Child

Strength: Although they can have some trouble understanding each other, Artisan parents can be valuable role models for their Idealist children. Little Idealists tend to get lost in imagination, in *what's possible*, and the Artisan's warm embrace of *what is* can set an important example for them. Artisans are in touch with reality, free in physical action, comfortable with their bodies, not worried about who they are—and this easygoing way in life can help give balance to the soulful, intense, self-searching Idealist child.

Weakness: On the other hand, this difference can present problems. Artisan parents have trouble sympathizing with their Idealist children's high-flown imagination, and they might tease them for being so head-in-the-clouds, or so lost in fantasy. In the worst case, they might even tell their Idealist kids to toughen up and take hold of reality. For the most part, though, Artisan parents don't interfere with people they don't understand, and so they relate with their Idealist children with lenience, tolerance, and a sense of fun.

Artisan Parent—Rational Child

Strength: The relationship between Artisan parents and Rational children is often happy and productive. The Artisan parents' hands-off style is perfect for little Rational individualists, who want no hands put on them. Also, both parent and child have a strong desire to do *what works*, so they can enjoy learning skills, sharing tools, and building things. But even more important, Artisan parents can help their Rational kids learn to flex their muscles and take some risks now and then. Rational youngsters need to put down their schoolbooks and library books, their computers and video games, and take time to develop their body. Artisan parents, with their courage and athleticism, can make it much easier for their Rational kids to overcome their fear of failure and enjoy getting physical.

Weakness: Rational children often puzzle their Artisan parents, who cannot understand their youngsters' avid interest in books and studies, particularly concerning theoretical subjects such as math and science. The Artisan parent's attitude is "why not get out in the world and learn a trade?" or "why not get your nose out of that book and have some fun?" But such misunderstandings are usually overshadowed by the Artisan parent and Rational child's shared enjoyment of the latest tools and technologies.

Traditional Guardians

Guardians have a traditional parenting style, believing that their job is to take their children firmly in hand and raise them to be responsible adults. They want to make sure their kids behave politely, with good manners, and with respect for authority and property. They want their youngsters to become hard workers, to take their duties seriously, and to fulfill their obligations. And they want their children to learn, and to follow, the rules and customs of society. Guardians take their parental duty seriously and do everything they can to instill these traditional values in their children, values which can pretty well be summed up by the twelve points of Boy Scout law: children are to be trustworthy, loyal, helpful, friendly, courteous, kind, obedient, cheerful, thrifty, clean, brave, and reverent.

Discipline: Guardian parents can be strict with their kids, believing that physical punishment is the best way to teach children how to behave—to spare the rod, they assume, is to spoil the child. And if not spanking, then at least scolding is the way to get their kids' attention and set them on the right path. But if Guardians get after their children, they do so because they love them dearly and want them to lead good honest lives. And if they're strict, they're also conscientious about caring for their children, seeing to it that they are well fed, clothed, and sheltered, even willing to sacrifice their own comforts to make sure their kids are safe and sound.

Film Portrait: Carol Connelly (Helen Hunt) in *As Good As It Gets*

Guardian Parent—Artisan Child

Strength: In most cases Guardian parents and their Artisan children get along just fine. Both call the real world home, so they speak the same language of *what is*, even though the Guardian parent is usually trying to settle things down, and the Artisan child is usually trying to shake things up. Guardian parents are particularly valuable when these kids are young, a short leash being just what mischievous little Artisans need.

Weakness: When their Artisan children get into their teens, Guardian parents can run into a buzz saw. Artisan children want to be free, excited, and bold, yet now their Guardian parents expect them to be grown up, responsible, and respectful. The scoldings and spankings that worked when the children were little now backfire, sometimes badly. Young Artisans, in their rebellion against a strict Guardian parent, may get into trouble with drugs, or sex, or with the law. Much of this can be avoided if Guardian parents will support their Artisan children in productive activities—playing sports, joining a band, working on cars—that let them shine in physical action.

Guardian Parent—Guardian Child

Strength: With children of their own temperament, Guardian parents have a relatively easy time of it. Parent and child both inhabit the world of *what is*, and both value doing *what's right*—in other words, what's allowed, what pleases others, or what's expected of them. In fact, Guardian children rarely have a rebellious period, but seem born to trust in authority, to follow the rules, and to be responsible, thus fitting hand in glove with their Guardian parents.

Weakness: Guardian children are instinctively cautious and prone to worry, and Guardian parents can reinforce these fears and concerns without knowing it. Guardian kids would do well if one of their parents were more carefree and optimistic. In addition, especially strict Guardian parents can want their children to be quiet and humble—to be seen and not heard—but such demands only further inhibit little Guardians, who are overcontrolled to begin with, and who often need loosening up to develop their self-confidence.

Guardian Parent—Idealist Child

Strength: Guardian parents have few problems with their Idealist children. Since Idealist kids are given to doing *what's right*, Guardian parents usually don't have to fight with them about following the rules and respecting authority. Idealist children care about doing what's expected of them—doing well at school, going to church, helping others, etc.—and so can be a great source of pride for their Guardian parents.

Weakness: Guardian parents live in the real world of *what is*, which can sometimes make communication pretty difficult with their fantasy-filled, *what's possible* Idealist children. Guardians often have no idea why their little Idealists are so dreamy and faraway, and they can worry that something might even be wrong with them. Then when their kids get to be teenagers and begin voicing their ivory-towered social and political views, Guardian parents can wonder what on earth has come over them. Also, little do Guardian parents know how irritating it is when they remind their Idealist kids to be good and do what they're told. Idealist children are good to begin with, and don't need to be reminded. This sort of parenting is not always bad for Idealist children, but it can weaken the relationship, sometimes pushing the children into rebellious behavior, just to establish their identity.

Guardian Parent—Rational Child

Strength: Guardian parents look on with approval at their Rational children's seriousness and need-to-achieve, on the surface so much like their own sense of concern and dedication to their work. Guardians also set a good example for their Rational kids, showing them the satisfactions of a full social and family life. And Guardians with their feet on the ground provide a valuable foundation for their lost-in-space Rational youngsters. In fact, this relationship works out quite well, provided that Guardian parents show regard for their little Rationals' fierce sense of autonomy.

Weakness: But there's the rub. Rational kids want to be free to choose for themselves, and when Guardian parents try to control them, the relationship can turn into a power struggle. Rational kids also want reasons for what they're asked to do, and when Guardian parents rely only on rules and authority, little Rationals will often refuse to cooperate. Now, Rational kids always prefer to do *what works*, and so they might do what they're told in order to avoid trouble. But they will comply in this way only reluctantly and with little respect. And Guardian parents are ill-advised to try to scold or punish their Rational children into obeying—especially to spank them. Little Rationals will feel personally violated and will likely respond with powerful and lasting resentment. Fortunately, Guardians frequently marry Artisans, and having this live-and-let-live parent in the mix can rescue Rational children from the sometimes heavy hand of Guardian discipline.

Bonding Idealists

Idealist parents can be called "bonding" in the sense that they strive to form close, loving personal relationships with their children. They love to hug their kids (surely it was an Idealist who started the "Have you hugged your child today?" campaign), but even more important is heart-to-heart emotional connection. Idealist parents are vitally interested in their kids' personal development, and they begin talking with them from a very early age, especially about their youngsters' hopes and dreams, their fears and fantasies. More than providing a good home, Idealist parents want to help their children feel good about themselves, to develop a positive self-image, and they hope in the process to create a special relationship with their kids—more like two good friends than a parent and child.

Discipline: This desire to be friends with their children can sometimes get in the way of discipline. When their kids act up, Idealist parents often have difficulty setting limits and sticking to their guns. They hate to be the "bad guy" in disputes with their youngsters, having to come down hard and enforce the limits firmly. And so instead of holding their position, Idealists will often try to settle things by acting as counselors with their children or, at the very least, as patient, understanding listeners. Actually, Idealists try to create this same harmony in the whole family. Wanting everyone to get along, they take on the role of family diplomat or peacekeeper, trying to make sure that all family members are happy and fulfilled, that all emotional needs are being met, and that kindness prevails—an impossible task that can cause them a good deal of grief. Fortunately, the Idealists' love for their family is boundless, and they will overcome every difficulty with renewed enthusiasm.

Film Portrait: Maria von Trapp (Julie Andrews) in *The Sound of Music*

Idealist Parent—Artisan Child

Strength: Idealist parents are enthusiastic supporters of their Artisan children's artistic interests. Idealists love the arts, and have often had their own try at music, acting, dancing, and the like, although they tend to be more introspective than spontaneous in their artistry. And so when there comes into the family a little Artisan who is instinctively drawn to an instrument, to the stage, or to the studio—and who seems to have such natural, effortless abilities—the Idealist parent is happy and proud to help the child reach the highest level possible. While this is less true with Artisan kids who are into sports, crafts, and trades, Idealist parents are natural-born nurturers, and will do everything they can to make sure their Artisan children reach their true potential.

Weakness: Idealist parents are unlike their Artisan children in both Saying and Doing. Artisan kids live for *what is*, happily racing from one physical action to another, with hardly a trace of intuition or make-believe. And Artisan kids are into *what works*, clever in getting what they want, and not very concerned with the ethics or fairness of their actions. Because of these basic differences, Idealist parents can be disappointed by their Artisan children's lack of interest in fantasy and heartfelt sharing, and by their lack of conscience and cooperation with family members. Wanting their relationships with their children to be deep and meaningful, sincere and harmonious, Idealist parents can feel a little let down when the relationship does not grow in those directions, but remains more a matter of caregiving and discipline than of soulful bonding.

Idealist Parent—Guardian Child

Strength: Since Idealist parents and Guardian children both have a basic desire to do *what's right*, they have a healthy respect for each other's sense of fair play, honesty, integrity, truthfulness—in short, for each other's need to live with a conscience. Also, these parents and children both greatly value a close-knit family, and so can count on each other's spirit of cooperation, kindness, sympathy, and willingness to help other members of the family get along together.

Weakness: Idealist parents, with their eye on potentials—on *what's possible*—can have trouble accepting their Guardian children's concrete *what is* nature. They keep looking for a sense of fantasy in their little Guardians, hoping that they are going to develop the powerful love of make-believe the parents value so deeply. Idealist parents may even put some gentle pressure on their Guardian children to follow the Idealist path in this regard. For example, Idealist parents often have favorite books of fairy tales they want to read to their children, stories they're sure will inspire their child's sense of wonder. But most Guardian kids would really rather be playing with their toys and games and friends, and so their parents' interest in fantasy really doesn't have much chance to take root.

Idealist Parent—Idealist Child

Strength: Idealist parents find a deep satisfaction with their Idealist children, who after all are born with their parent's two most valued traits of character. First, little Idealists have a budding sense of wonder about *what's possible*: they are filled with imagination, they love fantasy and make-believe, they are spellbound by stories (and will make up stories themselves), they show remarkable empathy for other people, and they seem to enjoy talking over ideas and playing with words—all to the delight of their Idealist parents. At the same time, Idealist children most often look to do *what's right*: they have respect for rules (even if they don't always follow them), they are sensitive to others' feelings, and they do all they can to create family harmony. If any parent-child relationship could be called soulful, it's this one.

Weakness: And yet Idealist parents and children sometimes rub each other the wrong way. Quite often thin-skinned, Idealists can be touchy and sharp with other people—their convictions might be deep-seated, but their emotions are very near the surface. And when the beliefs or the feelings of Idealist parents and children come into conflict, with each holding fast to his or her ideals, they can hardly avoid irritating each other. These are usually quick flare-ups, however, with both parent and child more interested in soothing the hurt and restoring good relations than in holding a grudge.

Idealist Parent—Rational Child

Strength: Idealist parents can form especially strong ties with their Rational children. Little Rationals share with these parents the love of ideas—the fascination with *what's possible*—and so the two meet happily when it's story time, with both loving tales of mythic heroes, of noble quests, and of wizardry and magic. And when their Rational children get a bit older, Idealist parents thoroughly enjoy family discussions with them, thrilled to see their child's curiosity, ingenuity, and logic at work as they frame arguments and try to express their complex ideas. Rational kids often need help with words and sentences, and Idealist parents can help them a great deal by showing them how to communicate more effectively. And Idealist parents are also a good role model in another way: with their warm and affectionate nature, they can bring out the loving side in Rational children, and help teach them how to find happiness in close personal relationships.

Weakness: And yet this match has a down side as well. Idealist parents can be dismayed by their Rational child's calm pragmatism and self-sufficiency—their focus on doing *what works*, and their attitude of needing no one else to be happy. These perfectly normal Rational traits can seem cold, even cruel, to Idealist parents, who prefer warm, friendly, cooperative family relations, and who sometimes feel it's their duty to help their Rational youngsters learn to be more kind and considerate, and to develop more of a conscience. Needless to say, Rational children aren't about to change their ways, and Idealist parents soon learn that they need to let their little Rationals alone, and appreciate them for being the strong individuals they are.

Individualist Rationals

It's of paramount importance to Rational parents that their children become independent and self-sufficient. Children are to be, and to be treated as, individuals, responsible to themselves alone for building successful lives. Make no mistake, Rational parents stand ready to help their kids in reaching their goals, whatever they might be. But they are reluctant to interfere with them and do for them, even if they see them foundering a bit. Children who are saved from failure can become dependent on others, and Rationals have little patience with neediness or dependence in their kids. They figure that if they are honest with their children, and respect them as individuals, they will turn out fine in the long run.

Discipline: When Rational parents do have to step in and take a hand with their kids, they often use what Keirsey calls the "abuse-it-lose-it" method of discipline. Rationals regard most of the things their children get to do as privileges rather than rights: eating with the family, talking to adults, playing with toys, enjoying the family pet, and so on. And Rationals seem to know instinctively that, when their child abuses one of these privileges—refuses to eat, say, or hits the dog—all they need to do is rescind the privilege immediately and unconditionally for a set period of time, making sure not to comment on the child's behavior. Unlike spanking, scolding, counseling, or even reasoning with their kids, this method does not put the child down as being wrong or "bad." The child simply loses the privilege, no questions asked, and it's his or her choice to regain it by acting differently. Now this is the most effective way for parents to set limits for their kids, but it is not very easy, even for Rationals.

Film Portrait: Atticus Finch (Gregory Peck) in *To Kill a Mockingbird*

Rational Parent—Artisan Child

Strength: Rationals make probably the best parents for Artisan children. Both are interested in doing *what works,* and so Rationals not only get a kick out of how clever their Artisan kids can be with tools, but they're also happy to support them in whatever kind of artistic activity calls to them, no matter if it's sports, music, theater, mechanics, or what have you. In addition, doing *what works* gives Rational parents just the right approach to handling little Artisans. These children can be wild and rebellious, and need firm limits to corral them and quiet them down. They do not want to hear what's the *right* thing to do, and they do not take well to spanking or scolding. Fortunately, Rational parents have a knack for the "abuse-it-lose-it" method, which lays no moral messages onto their little

Artisans. The naturally practical and adaptable Artisan child does not fight the reality of such clear, "no strings attached" limits, and soon plays happily within the boundaries.

Weakness: Although Rational parents try to stay pretty objective about their kids, and not impose expectations on them, they can feel a twinge of disappointment with the mostly physical nature of their Artisan children. Rationals value their own outlook on life—calm, abstract, logical, skeptical—and when they see that their Artisan children are reckless and impulsive, going headlong into any activity that excites them, they can begin to wonder "Why me?" But Rational parents quickly accept that their Artisan youngster is probably not going to become a serious little scientist buried in technical books, and they take their satisfaction from encouraging the child's individuality.

Rational Parent—Guardian Child

Strength: Rational parents do just fine with their Guardian children, even though they have neither of the basic dimensions of personality in common. What they do share is a serious attitude toward work. Little Guardians are extremely responsible in their schoolwork, and they are thorough, hard-working, and uncomplaining when given tasks or chores around the house. These traits make a good fit with the studious, work-compulsive Rational parent.

Weakness: Rational parents have to be careful not to let slip any hint of dissatisfaction with their Guardian children for being so completely different from them. First, since Guardian kids live in the literal, concrete world of *what is*, they aren't that interested in either the story books or the theoretical subjects that their Rational parents find so valuable—and thus the vital connection of pondering *what's possible* probably won't be very strong. Second, Rational parents can wonder about their Guardian child's tendency to follow along. Guardian youngsters like to do what's expected of them, and in their social life this means they will often follow fads and fashions, trying to fit in with their friends by doing what the other kids are doing. Now, unless they're careful, Rational parents, so strong in their individuality and autonomy, can easily send their Guardian kids the message that wanting to be like the other kids is somehow a trivial pursuit.

Rational Parent—Idealist Child

Strength: Rational parents are both fascinated and delighted with the enthusiasm and imagination of their Idealist children. The two temperaments are both interested in *what's possible*, and so relating through fantasy stories, make-believe, word games, and the like comes naturally to them. And when Idealist youngsters get into high school, and are brimming with ideas and opinions about the books they've read, Rational parents eagerly join into discussions with them. Such mutual delight in books and ideas is the basis of a strong bond of love between Rational parents and Idealist children, one that usually lasts a lifetime.

Weakness: Rational parents, confident they can handle their children by *doing what works*, can be thrown for a loop by their *do what's right* Idealist child. To be sure, the Rational's favorite "abuse-it-lose-it" method of discipline, which rescinds an abused privilege for a set period of time without comment, does not always work with highly emotional Idealist kids. Sometimes it can actually backfire by making the little Idealist feel treated impersonally, without a chance to explain his or her actions. Nor does the Idealist child respond well to the Rational parent's other preferred methods: logical explanation and calm persuasion. Even allowing natural (or logical) consequences to correct their behavior is not that effective with Idealist youngsters, even though this might quiet them down in the end. Given neither to scolding nor to spanking their children, Rational parents quickly learn that the thing to do with irate little Idealists is to back off and quietly observe them, letting the fire of temper burn itself out.

Rational Parent—Rational Child

Strength: Rational parents have little, if any, difficulty in dealing with their Rational children. Reasoning with most kids is like shouting into the wind, but little Rationals will listen to reason, and the older they get the more they will listen. So Rational parents can relax, knowing that if they are reasonable in their requirements and messages, their Rational children will respond in kind. Also, with the same styles of saying *what's possible* and doing *what works*, Rational parents delight in many of their Rational children's traits, but particularly in their love of fantasy, their individuality, and their curiosity.

Rational children can't get enough stories about heroes and wizards triumphing over evil tyrants; they are born insisting on their independence; and they can become almost single-minded in their efforts to learn about science and technology, and to sharpen the many tool skills they take as their points of pride.

Weakness: Rational parents might enjoy seeing their own characteristics mirrored in their offspring, but they must also recognize their Rational child's need for social development. Better for Rational children to have at least one Artisan, Guardian, or Idealist parent who can show them how to have some fun, how to enjoy friends and family, or how to get along with others.

The Pygmalion Parent

Keirsey stresses that the Pygmalion Project, so common in mating, is even more of a temptation in parenting. Most parents believe quite sincerely that their responsibility is to *raise* their children, to take an active part in guiding them, or perhaps in steering them, on their way to becoming adults. This seems almost like part of the job description of Mother or Father. Unfortunately, such a proactive, hands-on model of parental responsibility—well-intentioned though it might be—all too often ends in family struggle.

The problem is that well-meaning parents tend to act on two questionable assumptions:

(1) they believe their children are pretty much the same as they are, chips off the old block; or

(2) they see kids as pieces of clay that will take whatever shape they are given.

But the truth is that kids are most likely quite different from their parents, and they will develop in widely different directions, no matter what their parents do to influence them one way or the other. Keirsey makes it clear that parents who assume they know what their kids want or need, think or feel, are usually quite wrong. And he argues that parents who see children as moldable clay fail to realize that, from the beginning, their kids are very much their own persons—Artisans, Guardians, Idealists, or Rationals—and that no amount of shaping them up can change their inborn structure.

What then are parents to do? Essentially, Keirsey advises parents to become child watchers, not child shapers. Parents need to let nature take its course by giving their children ample room to grow into their true character, and they should play an active role only when they see an opportunity to encourage growth that fits in with their child's temperament. In short, parents need to learn how to support their children in becoming what they were born to be.

5

Talent and Career

Premiering on September 8, 1966, spanning five television series, spinning off nine movies—and still going strong—Gene Roddenberry's *Star Trek* has proven to be one of the most popular and durable sagas in entertainment history. The reasons for this success are many, but two stand out here. Certainly the interplay of strong and distinctive personalities in the various crews has been a treat to watch over the years. But it's also been fascinating to see these different kinds of characters, all highly skilled at their jobs, teaming their different talents in a common enterprise.

Now, temperament styles in *Star Trek* are not all over the map, even though Starfleet employs several alien races and the voyages take us to every quadrant of the galaxy. In fact, if we look for patterns of personality among the different casts and crews, Keirsey's four temperaments emerge in sharp relief, almost as if written into the very character descriptions.

• **Artisans** abound in *Star Trek*—after all, it's about "boldly going where no one has gone before." Artisans are the adventurers in the stories: impulsive, resourceful, risk-taking, not bound by rules and regulations, and usually having an eye for the opposite sex. The original was **Capt. James T. Kirk**, explorer, fighter, lover, and a legend at being able to think on his feet and come up with some clever scheme or maneuver to save his ship and crew from certain disaster. But there's also the ace mechanic Scotty, the sensual, fearless weapons expert Tasha Yar, the top gun pilot Tom Paris, the shrewd entrepreneur Quark, and the newest Artisan, the impetuous, insubordinate, good-natured Capt. Jonathan Archer.

• **Guardians** act as a stabilizing counterweight to these gung ho space cowboys in *Star Trek*. Guardians are usually the ship's doctors and security officers, concerned with defending the crew from danger and disease. They are cautious, traditional people who respect the rules and who are usually shy and a bit awkward around the opposite sex. **Dr. Leonard McCoy** ("Bones") the steady, crusty, commonsense country doctor established the type, but the protective Beverly Crusher and the fastidious, long-suffering EMH are of similar stripe. As for security officers, the yardstick is the stern, ritualistic, and honor bound **Mr. Worf**, but think also of the gruff, wary Odo, and the newest Guardian, the by-the-book Lt. Malcolm Reed.

• **Idealists** are the source of emotional wellness, spirituality, and personal diplomacy in the stories. The first Idealist in *Star Trek* was ship's counselor **Deanna Troi**, an empath whose ability to read others' feelings brought a new dimension of personality to the Next Generation. Troi was joined by Guinan with her prescience and ageless wisdom, then followed by Benjamin Sisco on his journey of enlightenment, by Julian Bashir with his quiet romanticism and love of humanity, by Chakotay with his vision quests, by Kes the gentle spirit and healer (who evolves into a beam of light), and finally by the latest Idealist, Dr. Phlox, a cheerful mystic who heals his patients with exotic medicine and a healthy dose of enthusiasm.

• **Rationals** provide the voice of reason and technological know-how in *Star Trek*. The prototype is, of course, **Mr. Spock**, the Vulcan science officer famous for his calm observation, precise data, and impeccable logic. But other Rationals include the ever-curious android science officer Data, the remote, analytical Capt. Jean-Luc Picard, and the tough-minded Capt. Kathryn Janeway, a brilliant physicist whose hero is Leonardo da Vinci. Then there is the headstrong master engineer B'Elanna Torres, the tactless and ruthlessly efficient 7-of-9, the austere and self-disciplined Tuvok, and the newest Rational, 'TPol, another quietly logical Vulcan science officer who is assigned to observe what her people call the "primitive and irrational" human beings.

Adventurers, Defenders, Counselors, and Scientists: each *Star Trek* crew shows us four kinds of personality living and working together on the most challenging and dangerous missions. Their very survival depends not only upon their bonds of friendship, but upon the contributions of their four types of talent.

Temperament, Talent, and Work

David Keirsey's terms for the four types of talent have a bit of a Starfleet ring to them, probably because he flew in the military himself, as a Marine fighter pilot in the Pacific in World War II. In Keirsey's view, the four temperament styles consistently demonstrate four general kinds of talent, called in military terms: Tactical, Logistical, Diplomatic, and Strategic. Further, Keirsey argues that these four talents tend to suit each temperament remarkably well to its own particular kind of work. Here are the matchups:

Temperament	Talent in	Work best with
Artisan	Tactics	Tools & Equipment
Guardian	Logistics	Supplies & Schedules
Idealist	Diplomacy	People & Communication
Rational	Strategy	Plans & Technologies

In general, this means that:

• **Artisans** are gifted in **tactical** work, using a variety of tools and operating all kinds of equipment to get things done right now.

• **Guardians** are outstanding in **logistical** work, handling supplies and establishing schedules in order to stabilize operations.

• **Idealists** shine in **diplomatic** work, helping people along the road of personal development and more effective communication.

• **Rationals** excel at **strategic** work, making plans and constructing technologies in order to achieve clearly thought out objectives.

But not only are the four temperaments superior in work that makes use of their natural gifts, they also find their greatest job satisfaction in doing what they do best. Thus Artisans get their kicks at work when they employ their physical skills and improvise in action. Guardians know they're contributing their best when they administer goods and services and enforce policies. Idealists feel inspired when they guide personal growth and help people work together. And Rationals get their greatest sense of accomplishment when they coordinate operations and engineer ways and means.

Of course, these connections between temperament, talent, and work have some crossover, with each temperament certainly able to do more than one kind of job. For example, Rational engineers, wizards in their labs and at their drawing tables, can also get pretty good at handling tools and building their inventions. In the same way, Artisan builders, crack with their power saws and arc-welders, can learn to do a good job of drawing simple construction blueprints. Although strategic and tactical jobs are far different, one person can certainly become competent at both.

Competent, but not usually expert. Why not? Because it takes more than effort or application to become truly expert at something. In most cases, expertise (brilliance, virtuosity) takes having a natural talent in an area, as well as the opportunity and the drive to develop that talent. Of course, not all of us can wait for a job that makes use of our best talent—we have to make a living. And not everyone will put in the long hours of practice needed to make the most of an inborn talent. But no matter what kind or level of job we settle for, the desire to do what comes naturally is strong within us.

This means that when a Guardian is hired as an engineer, he or she will put in long hours and do solid work, but will very likely look for promotion to some form of administration in the engineering department. On the other hand, when a Rational engineer is promoted to department head, he or she might be proud of the advancement, and might with time and effort become a decent administrator, but will very likely, sooner or later, lose interest and long to go back to the lab, even for less pay.

If possible, then, our best and most satisfying career choice is one that suits our greatest talent. And our talent is inextricably wound up with our temperament style. So let's look more closely at the four kinds of talent, and at the different kinds of jobs that fit the four temperaments.

Artisans: Making Things Happen

Artisan Talent

"Tactical" is the most visible of the four types of talent, because tactics are maneuvers that better a person's immediate position—that make things happen in the here and now. Agile in body and mind,

Artisans really have no peer when it comes to tactical moves. First, they have the inborn ability to pick up whatever tool, instrument, or piece of equipment that catches their eye, practice with it until they have mastered it, and then use it to get the results they want. But Artisans are also clever improvisers. They're always on the lookout for some better angle of approach, always scanning for some opening that gives them an advantage in action, or an edge on their competition. In other words, Artisans always keep an eye on where they want to go, and they instinctively come up with the fastest way to get there.

Artisan Education

In school Artisans do their best work in arts programs, in trade schools, or in applied or technical training classes where they can practice moves and techniques with the various tools, instruments, machines, and so on, that grab their interest. Artisans are usually bored when asked to sit still and study academic subjects such as the humanities or theoretical science. But give them the opportunity to work freeform with their hands and their senses, and watch them come alive. Remember, however, that "art" must not be limited to the fine arts, such as painting and sculpture, or the performing arts, such as acting and dance, but in fact includes the athletic, culinary, martial, mechanical, and industrial arts, not to mention what's been called the "art of the deal" in business.

Artisan Careers and Jobs

There are four general career fields that make good use of this talent for tactical maneuvering, and that therefore fit Artisans to a "T" (for Tactical):

Marketing in the broadest sense—doing whatever's needed to advance your commercial interests—comes easily to many Artisans. In government, business, sports, entertainment, etc., these Artisans know how to seize opportunities and to win people's confidence, and they use all their tactical skills to maneuver themselves, or their company, clients, products, etc., into the best possible position. Artisans who are good at, and enjoy, the rough and tumble game of "wheel and deal" will thrive in jobs such as:

- Advertising executive
- Concert promoter
- Contract negotiator
- Corporate recruiter
- Entrepreneur
- Lobbyist
- Marketing director
- Promotions manager

- Publicist/PR specialist
- Real estate developer
- Sales representative
- Show business producer
- Special events developer
- Stockbroker (high risk issues)
- Talent/Sports agent
- Travel agent

Toolwork has to do with the skillful handling of tools, implements, utensils, instruments, machinery, vehicles, and so on. Many Artisans are captivated by such devices, and often learn to use them with unbelievable mastery. Artisans who have this knack for working with "tools of the trade" should steer toward jobs such as:

- Appliance repair technician
- Carpenter
- Computer technician
- Construction worker
- Cook/Bartender
- Firefighter/Paramedic
- Heavy equipment operator
- Machinist/Metal worker

- Mechanic (cars, airplanes, etc.)
- Musician
- Pilot/Flight instructor
- Plumber/Electrician
- Police sharpshooter
- Potter/Weaver
- Surgeon
- Truck driver

Entertainment involves putting on a show of some kind in order to give pleasure to others. Many outgoing Artisans feel on stage wherever they are and love to be in the spotlight, improvising moves on the spot to charm their audience. Artisans who have this interest in people and this kind of spontaneous showmanship in their blood will show a real flair for jobs such as:

- Activities director
- Actor/Comedian
- Aerobics/Fitness instructor
- Auctioneer
- Corporate spokesperson
- Disc jockey
- Event emcee
- New product demonstrator

- Newscaster
- Resort social director
- Restaurateur
- Sales force trainer
- Singer/Dancer
- Sports announcer
- Talk show host
- Tour guide

101

Artwork is the job of artistic design, or in other words, the taking of sensory elements, ingredients, fragments (sounds, shapes, colors, textures, tastes, moves, and so on), and then fitting them together into attractive or striking arrangements—also called "works of art." Artisans who have an eye for this kind of artistic composition will have great fun expressing their creativity in jobs such as:

- Art director
- Beautician/Hair stylist
- Chef
- Choreographer
- Commercial artist
- Composer/Song writer
- Fashion/Costume designer
- Film/Stage director

- Film/Video editor
- Graphic artist
- Interior decorator
- Novelist/Playwright/Poet
- Painter/Sculptor
- Photographer
- Set designer
- Studio sound mixer

Artisans in Charge

Whatever career field they explore, when Artisans end up in charge they call the shots in their own style.

Strength: As managers, Artisans are both tactical and practical. Impatient with doing routine paperwork, keeping records, and writing goal statements, they greatly prefer to escape the office and deal with the troubles and emergencies of day-to-day operations. Artisan managers also usually know what's really going on in their workplace. They observe their people and operations close-up, and with a sharp eye, and so they quickly spot breakdowns as they occur—and they'll do whatever it takes to fix them. Artisans are adaptable, open-minded, and easy to get along with, welcoming new ideas and changing positions easily as new facts and new situations arise. Not interested in fighting the system or judging their employees, Artisan managers are at their best when improvising actions and making on-the-spot decisions, using the people and resources at hand to put out fires and to get operations back on line.

Weakness: Artisans tend to be impulsive, acting on the spur of the moment, and this can make them unpredictable managers. Living so fully in the here and now, Artisans can be careless about schedules, they can be unprepared at times when preparation is called for, and they can spring the unexpected on employees. Since current demands get all their attention, Artisan managers are liable to forget prior commitments and decisions, they sometimes fail to follow through on agreements, and they might even neglect to inform others of changes in assignment or schedule.

The truth is that for an organization of any size Artisans are incomparable in crisis situations that call for their amazing tactical skills. Keirsey calls them "Troubleshooters," and he advises that they be kept mobile and used only to get operations up and running, and to handle quick fixes when trouble arises.

Guardians: Minding the Store

Guardian Talent

The great talent of Guardians lies in "logistics," that is, in the care and keeping of supplies and schedules. Logistical routines might not be as flashy as tactical maneuvers, but they are just as important in keeping the workplace running smoothly. In order for any business or institution to function effectively—in order to get any difficult job done—schedules need to be set and met, procedures established and monitored, policies published and enforced; also supplies have to be gathered, stored, inventoried, and distributed; billing and taxes, payroll and benefits must be taken care of; equipment must be serviced and maintained in good working order; property must be secured, and people given a safe workplace. With their strong respect for authority, their belief in rules and regulations, and their sharp eye for "everything in its place," Guardians are invaluable in handling all of these tasks.

Guardian Education

Guardians do well in high school, and they often go on to college to earn their degrees and credentials—though many find their most valuable lessons in the real-world "school of hard knocks." Whatever their major in college, Guardians keep their eye on the practical advantages of learning about business and commerce. They fill the ranks of business schools (even taking night classes) where they show a gift for secretarial and clerical skills, and they flock to college business departments, where they excel in accounting and business administration. Also many ambitious Guardians go to law school, where they tend to specialize in business, tax, and insurance law.

Guardian Careers and Jobs

The logistical talent of Guardians—handling materiel and implementing rules and schedules—suits them perfectly to four general career areas:

Administration is the work of managing people and directing operations, keeping one eye on people's performance, and the other on the policies and procedures that govern their activities. This can be a tough and thankless job, since it means applying standards to people's work and pointing out whether they're meeting or falling short of the mark. Guardians who want to take on this supervisory responsibility will be excellent in jobs such as:

- Athletic director
- Business manager
- City manager
- Factory/Plant supervisor
- Funeral director
- General contractor
- Hospital administrator
- Judge
- Maitre d'hotel
- Museum curator
- Office manager
- Police/Fire chief
- Politician
- School principal
- Staff sergeant
- Supermarket manager

Regulation means taking a close look at people, products, and accounts to make sure that irregularities are spotted and corrected, and that company tolerances and legal standards are strictly and accurately observed. Guardians with an eye for quality control and regulatory compliance should look into jobs such as:

- Accountant/Auditor
- Admissions officer/Registrar
- Attorney (tax, contracts, anti-trust)
- Bank inspector
- Bookkeeper
- Building inspector
- Customs agent
- Escrow officer
- FDA/Health inspector
- Grant management specialist
- Immigration officer
- Insurance appraiser
- IRS agent
- Lab technician
- Property assessor
- Quality assurance inspector

Service & Supply has to do with providing companies and their employees with whatever goods and services they need—funds, furniture, food, office supplies, housing, equipment, clean up—to maintain the pace of operations and get the job done right. Guardians who are interested in supporting and outfitting institutions, and in serving people, will be likely to succeed in jobs such as:

- Banker/Loan officer
- Credit counselor
- Farmer/Rancher
- Flight attendant
- Guest services manager
- Librarian
- Paralegal
- Pharmacist
- Purchasing agent
- Real estate agent
- Receptionist
- Salesperson
- Schoolteacher
- Secretary
- Shipping agent
- Storekeeper

Security involves safeguarding people and property: seeing to the physical health and welfare of those in need of care, and making sure their homes, businesses, and communities are safe and sound. Guardians who are especially interested in protecting people and contributing to their well-being will find their niche in jobs such as:

- Air marshal
- Border Patrol agent
- Corrections officer
- Dentist/Orthodontist
- Estate planner
- Exterminator
- FBI agent
- Fish & Game warden
- Insurance agent
- Nurse
- Optometrist
- Physical therapist
- Police officer
- Public prosecutor
- Security guard
- Social worker

Guardians in Charge

Regardless of their career field, Guardians often rise to management positions—they end up running the store—and they do so with their own particular strengths and weaknesses.

Strength: With their interests so deeply rooted in material supply, inspection, maintenance, and security—in logistics—Guardian leaders tend to have a stabilizing and consolidating effect on their organizations. They are good at establishing routines, rules, and protocols, at drawing up schedules and timetables, and at following through on jobs until completion. They can be superdependable leaders and extraordinarily hard workers, thorough, steady, reliable, and orderly. They value contracts, administrative regulations, and strong institutional traditions. People under Guardian managers know that they can count on things remaining constant and familiar. They know that the workplace will be safe, and that policies and personnel will be kept in good order under the Guardian's watchful eye.

Weakness: Stabilization is a necessary stage in the life of any organization, but there is a tendency, after a time, for stability to go too far, and for organizations to become needlessly bureaucratic. Guardian managers can have a problem here; in their earnest wish for rules, regulations, and traditions, they tend to resist change, and so may set up a roadblock to healthy organizational growth. They can also be irritated by maverick, nonconformist employees, or those who disregard schedules and established procedures. If Guardians feel that employees are shirking their duties, or are questioning authority, their instinct is to call this to their attention. And they may do this publicly rather than privately, and occasionally with words which are excessively critical.

In short, Guardian managers are better at consolidating an organization than making changes or meeting crises. These "Stabilizers," as Keirsey calls them, are loyal to company policies and personnel and do their best to conserve company values and traditions. Before they agree to changes, Guardians will weigh the consequences—they always look before they leap—and then they will base their actions on sound judgment. At this point they are decisive in settling things, and can be counted on to follow through on commitments.

Idealists: Working with People

Idealist Talent

Idealists show their greatest talent in "diplomacy," which is to say they have a gift for working positively and sensitively with people and personal relationships, both in directing human development, and also in improving lines of communication. Idealists are incomparable at creating imaginative learning environments and at helping people talk more openly and honestly with each other. Teaching, counseling, pastoring, and social work come easily to them, and are highly intuitive pursuits for them. And in business Idealists can do wonders in recruiting, interviewing, training, tutoring, placing, advancing, and advising personnel. With their insight and enthusiasm, with their unmatched communication skills, and with their keen eye for human potentials, Idealists can come to have tremendous positive influence over others, often inspiring them to grow as individuals, and helping them to get along more happily with those around them.

Idealist Education

Idealists usually do exceptionally well in all levels of school, because as students they have an ideal combination of traits: they are sincerely interested in cooperating with their teachers and classmates, and they also develop early language skills. Even as young children Idealists have a burning passion for words, and they start reading and writing well before most other kids. With their verbal ability, high school is often easy for them, and they frequently go on to college, where they tend to study humanities, but they will choose any subject—literature, philosophy, theology, law, theater, creative writing, journalism—that involves expressing ideas through words. They also take up the social sciences, particularly psychology, sociology, and social anthropology, and many go on to take advanced degrees and to teach in any of these fields.

Idealist Careers and Jobs

With their talent for being diplomatic with people and words, Idealists do wonderfully well on four career paths:

Education, for Idealists, is not so much a matter of lecturing or instructing people, but involves dreaming up imaginative experiences that kindle in students a passion for learning, and that help them develop their unknown potentials. Idealists want to make a difference in people's lives, and those who have the confidence and imagination to take others on this quest for enlightenment will flourish in jobs such as:

- Child care director
- Corporate training facilitator
- Curriculum software trainer
- Director of education
- Drama coach/Dramaturge
- Editor (book, magazine)
- Educ. software developer
- Human resources manager
- Instructional designer
- Learning specialist
- Motivational speaker
- Seminar presenter
- Special education teacher
- Teacher/Professor
- Training team leader
- Youth services director

Guidance has to do with facilitating personal growth, conducting people along pathways of physical well-being and spiritual self-discovery in order to help them lead healthy, happy lives. Idealists with the insight and compassion to guide people on their life's journey—to feel well, to find themselves, and to explore their talents—will hear their calling in jobs such as:

- Career counselor
- Child welfare counselor
- Dietician/Nutritionist
- Holistic physician
- Life coach
- Mental health professional
- Minister/Priest/Rabbi
- Occupational therapist
- Pediatrician
- Psychiatrist
- Psychologist
- School counselor
- Speech/language therapist
- Stress reduction therapist
- Substance abuse counselor
- Yoga instructor

Advocacy is literally "giving voice" to ideas and feelings, views and beliefs, that people have trouble putting into words for themselves—all to try to improve understanding between people and to bring about justice. Idealists who want to take up issues, champion causes, and speak for others will be exceptional in jobs such as:

- Civil Rights attorney
- Consumer watchdog
- Customer service advocate
- Editorial columnist
- Environmental activist
- Independent film maker
- Interviewer
- Journalist/Correspondent
- Lecturer
- Missionary
- Novelist/Playwright
- Personnel recruiter
- Press secretary
- Public defender
- Speech writer
- TV documentary producer

Personal Relations is the field of human cooperation—of people learning to get along together in the workplace, the family, communities, and so on. Idealists who are sensitive to the strained relationships they find around them, and who are committed to resolving conflicts, reconciling differences, and building bridges between people will find enormous satisfaction in jobs such as:

- Adoptions coordinator
- Communications specialist
- Community relations director
- Conflict resolution attorney
- Dean of students
- Diplomat
- Diversity manager
- Family therapist
- Labor relations mediator
- Marriage counselor
- Personnel manager
- Social services liaison
- Social worker
- Student exchange coordinator
- Translator/Interpreter
- Tutor (language, writing, etc.)

Idealists in Charge

Having such strong people skills, Idealists often become leaders in their career field, where they manage people in their special way.

Strength: Idealists are first and foremost people-oriented, and they tend to become personally committed to the progress of their employees, staff, students, parishioners, and so on. Idealists are sympathetic, willing to listen to people's troubles, and are sincerely concerned with their personal problems. At the same time, they focus primarily on potentialities, always looking for and reacting to the best in their people, and always ready with a word of encouragement. This personal concern of Idealist managers—trying to understand and to help everyone under them—can be quite inspiring to their personnel, motivating them not only to make their very best effort, but also to work together in an atmosphere of mutual caring and respect.

Weakness: And yet the Idealist's personal touch can also have its liabilities. No doubt because of their close involvement with others, Idealists are often, even excessively, turned to for moral support and counsel, and they seem to have little defense against becoming caught up in other people's troubles. Also, by emphasizing only the positive accomplishments of their people, Idealists can ignore real personnel problems and weak points, and find that these have festered into serious issues. And if Idealists come under criticism themselves, including negative evaluations from either their superiors or their subordinates, they are liable to take such comments personally and can become quite discouraged.

These few shortcomings aside, Idealists can be extraordinary as the head of any group of people. They are visible, charismatic leaders who speak well for their organization and for the people in it. They are caring and enthusiastic leaders—Keirsey calls them "Inspirational" leaders—who focus on the good in people, and who welcome contributions from one and all.

Rationals: Figuring Things Out

Rational Talent

The "strategic" talent of Rationals can be defined as the ability to figure out complex plans to achieve well-defined, long-range goals. These strategic plans can be command structures and directives that coordinate projects, or they can be blueprints and paradigms for engineering systems. But whatever Rationals set their mind to, their aim is always to advance efficiently toward their goal. To this end, Rationals look far ahead and all around, envisioning how an organization will look in the future, how its personnel and products will fare in the long haul; and they take in all relevant information, all pertinent data, so that their plans for growth and innovation leave nothing important to chance. And owing to the clarity of their vision, and to the logic of their ways and means, Rationals are often able to interest people with their plans for the future, and to enlist support for their leadership.

Rational Education

It is hard to get Rationals to study subjects that are not in some way connected to math, science, or philosophy. In essence, Rationals want to know how complex systems work, whether organic systems (like plants, animals, and galaxies), mechanical systems (like computers, aircraft, and telecommunications), social systems (like families, businesses, and economies), or cognitive systems (like logic and epistemology). Now, learning about systems is the work of science, requiring logical investigation, objective experimentation, mathematical description, and reasoned debate. And so in high school Rationals take all the science, math, and computer classes they can find. Then in college they major in the physical sciences and the social sciences, but also in computer science, mathematics, economics, and engineering—often with a philosophy minor. And they enroll in huge numbers in graduate degree programs in any of these subjects.

Rational Careers and Jobs

The Rationals' talent in strategic planning gives them considerable advantage in four general career categories:

Leadership in any kind of enterprise (commercial, educational, political, military, and so on) has to do with setting and then executing a strategic plan—first by quickly designating the tasks to be accomplished, and then by mobilizing the forces and resources, the personnel and materiel, that will most efficiently achieve the goals. Rationals with the assertiveness and decisiveness to take command in this way will be outstanding in jobs such as:

- Athletic director
- Business executive/CEO
- Campaign manager
- College dean
- Conductor/Music director
- Corporate team leader
- Film director
- International financier
- Management consultant
- Military commander
- Politician
- Public works commissioner
- School superintendent
- Senior litigation attorney
- Sports franchise GM
- Venture capitalist

Coordination involves gathering data, figuring out the sequence of jobs to be done, and arranging people and schedules in the most efficient way possible—that is, to get the maximum productivity with a minimum waste of time and resources. Often this requires making contingency plans for keeping projects on track, "if-then" alternatives designed to deal with foreseeable errors and shortages. Rationals with an eagle eye for knowing what they want done, when it must be done, who can best do it, and what can go wrong will be invaluable in jobs such as:

111

- Computer analyst
- Construction project manager
- Curriculum designer
- Data-stream manager
- Efficiency expert
- Ergonomics engineer
- Forensic criminologist
- Human factors consultant
- Method validation specialist
- Network integrator
- Personnel systems designer
- Production designer
- Research scientist
- Sociologist
- Stategic alliance coordinator
- Urban planner

Engineering is the work of inventing and constructing new and complex technologies with one practical function in mind: to make systems work more efficiently. Rationals who are looking to exercise their technological ingenuity—to build a better mousetrap—need to keep their sites set on jobs such as:

- Building consultant
- Chemist (product development)
- Entrepreneur
- Formulations scientist
- Genetic engineer
- Hardware systems designer
- Inventor
- Manufacturing technologist
- Mechanical engineer
- Oceanographer
- Performance analyst
- Physicist (mechanics, kinetics)
- Pilot project developer
- Prototype designer
- Software design engineer
- Structural dynamics analyst

Structural Design is the making of plans, blueprints, and models for building much of the complex infrastructure and technology that surrounds us, but also for designing new theoretical systems in the social sciences, mathematics, the physical sciences, and even in business and the humanities. Rationals with this desire to redesign the world more coherently will excel in jobs such as:

- Anthropologist
- Astronomer
- Construction architect
- Computer scientist
- Corporate strategist
- Economist
- Futurist
- Information analyst
- Investment strategist
- Logician
- Mathematician
- Philosopher
- Political scientist
- Psychologist
- Systems analyst
- Theoretical physicist

Rationals in Charge

Rationals have such a powerful drive to achieve and to advance in their careers that they often rise to positions of power in their organizations. When on top, they run things in a way all their own.

Strength: Rationals are the agents of strategic change. Always on the lookout for new and more productive ways of doing things, Rationals are often pioneers in technical and academic innovation. They define their goals clearly and they question all traditional rules, procedures, and offices, keeping only those that efficiently serve their ends. With their ability to see factors and coordinates with x-ray vision, they are extraordinary at planning and implementing new operating systems. With their sure grasp of the interworkings of systems and subsystems, they understand the long and short-term implications of the changes they propose. And using assessment methods such as systems analysis and flow-charting, they provide their organizations with a powerful view of things to come, together with an overall strategy for accomplishing goals.

Weakness: Because of their focus on long-range objectives—the big picture—Rationals can, at times, be unaware of their people's feelings, and may seem remote and uncaring. Rationals have little skill in the art of appreciation, and will usually show some impatience with errors—they cannot bear for either themselves or others to make the same mistake twice. Making matters worse, Rationals can become too technical in the way they talk, using highly specialized terminology to present enormously difficult concepts. Rationals aren't much good at small talk in the first place, and their high tech vocabulary and precise way of discussing ideas make it difficult for them to communicate with others on a personal level, which can leave them isolated from the people in their organization.

Despite their interpersonal blind spots, Rationals are Keirsey's "Visionary" leaders because they have the invaluable ability to envision the goals of an organization, and then to conceive strategic plans for accomplishing those goals. Ingenious, innovative, efficient, and proud of their technical know-how, Rationals are unmatched at forging chains of command, at mapping out contingency plans, at getting models onto paper, and at building prototypes—all to rise to challenges of technological progress.

Find Your Bliss

Joseph Campbell, the mythologist who in the 1980s was the subject of Bill Moyers' series *The Power of Myth* on Public Television, coined a phrase that might well sum up David Keirsey's views of temperament and career. Campbell said in an interview that the key to career satisfaction, and to career advancement as well, was to "find your bliss." Now, Keirsey might call it "matching talent to task," and modern slang might put it something more like "do your own thing," but the point is the same: if a person finds a career that makes use of his or her best talent, then that career will be a true pleasure, and doors will start to open.

But where do we start looking? This is where Keirsey's ideas on temperament can help. Keirsey's great contribution to career placement is that he has identified the innate talents of the four temperaments, and thus the job skills that come most easily to them. And so, armed with knowledge of their temperament, people have a much better idea of the kind of work they're cut out for, and therefore a much better chance of choosing the career that's right for them.

To sum up:

• **Artisans** are **tactical**, best at making free moves that get quick results, improvising in the moment to promote enterprises, to handle emergencies, and to help people have fun along the way.

• **Guardians** are **logistical**, best at administering goods and services, carefully scheduling times, places, and personnel for regular tasks, and reliably supporting and protecting people and property.

• **Idealists** are **diplomatic**, best at guiding people in their personal development, and at nurturing good relations, health, and high morale in their families, among their colleagues, and in the work force.

• **Rationals** are **strategic**, best at envisioning an organization's future, directing research and development, and organizing the design and construction of evolving projects.

May the Fource Be with You

The name of Joseph Campbell brings to mind another popular modern mythology developed in American science fiction, not in

Star Trek this time, but in George Lucas's film, *Star Wars* (1977). Lucas has said that his plot in *Star Wars* was influenced by Campbell's book *The Hero With a Thousand Faces*, a study of the archetypal hero's journey recounted again and again in most of the world's ancient mythologies. But maybe without knowing it, Lucas also appears to have been influenced by temperament theory, and it's more accurate to say that his heroes in *Star Wars* come with four faces:

• **Han Solo** is a hotheaded, risk-taking, freelance smuggler, also an ace pilot, a blaster master, and a high-stakes gambler. Escaping from the Imperial stormtroopers on the planet Tatooine, Han speaks like a true tactical **Artisan**: "We'll be safe enough once we make the jump to hyperspace. Besides, I know a few maneuvers. We'll lose them. Here's where the fun begins."

• **C-3PO** is a loyal, hard-working protocol droid, a touch of comic relief in *Star Wars* with his worries about the dangers and discomforts he faces, but also a key figure in the Rebellion, helping to deliver the Death Star plans to the Rebels. Sending his friend R2-D2 off to fight the Imperial forces, C-3PO voices his **Guardian** concern: "Hang in tight. You've got to come back. You wouldn't want my life to be boring, would you?" And when R2-D2 returns badly banged up and in need of repair, C-3PO shows his true-blue logistical colors: "If any of my circuits or gears would help, I'd gladly donate them."

• **Luke Skywalker**, as his name suggests, is a romantic dreamer, and also heir to the mystical Jedi Knights, the benevolent champions of the Republic and ministers of the Force—the spiritual life energy that binds the galaxy together. Once Luke decides "to learn the ways of the Force and become a Jedi like my father," he begins an **Idealist**'s journey to find both the wisdom and the power of human intuition, learning to "let go your conscious self," to "stretch out with your feelings" and to "trust your feelings."

• **Princess Leia** is a dynamic, strong-minded **Rational**, once a bright young Imperial Senator on Alderaan working to bring about reform, but now one of the leaders of the Rebel Alliance. Leia has every confidence that, in the long run, personal freedom will win out over tyranny, as she tries to explain to the Death Star commandant: "The more you tighten your grip, Tarkin, the more star systems will slip through your fingers." She risks her life to save "The technical read-outs of that battle station," and like any good Rational she puts her trust in strategic analysis: "I only hope that when the data's analyzed, a weakness can be found."

In the end, of course, a fatal weakness is found in the Death Star and Good triumphs over Evil—but let's not forget that it takes more than just one Force to win the day. Lucas's point in *Star Wars*, and certainly Keirsey's in *Please Understand Me II*, is that to succeed in complex enterprises we need the forces of all four temperaments: the force of daring action, the force of faithful service, the force of human feelings, and the force of strategic vision.

Appendix

The Sixteen Types

Although David Keirsey focuses on the four temperaments in *Please Understand Me II*, he also recognizes that there are unmistakable individual differences among the temperaments, and he goes on to discuss four distinct kinds of Artisans, Guardians, Idealists, and Rationals. The personality type portraits in this Appendix are simplified versions of what Keirsey calls the "role variants" of his temperaments. (Since my Shorter Sorter in Chapter 2 uses the Jung/Myers letters for scoring purposes, I'll include them here in the portrait headings as a means of identification.)

Four Artisans

Artisans, remember, are the *action* temperament, the operators and entertainers who most often speak about *what is* and who look to do *what works*. But Artisans also have some vital differences in how and where they make their moves.

Promoters (ESTP)

Of all the Artisans, Promoters are the most **engaging**, able to put forward an enterprise or a venture, and then to win people's confidence and persuade them to get on board. These are the **smooth** operators who handle people with much the same skill as other Artisans operate a variety of tools and instruments. People almost seem like musical **instruments** in their hands; Promoters pick them up gracefully, learn their stops quickly, and most often get them to play their tune.

There are lots of Promoters (just about 10% of the population), and life is never dull around them. They live in the **moment** and bring high **energy** wherever they go—when a Promoter enters the room, the lights come on, the music plays, the games begin. Promoters are **playful**, fun-loving people, calling attention to themselves by their charm and wit, and delighting their friends with their quips, stories, and jokes. Promoters are also **high rollers** who have a hearty appetite for the finer things in life—the new shows, the best food and wine, expensive cars, and stylish clothes. And they are extremely **sophisticated** in social circles, knowing many people by name, and able to say just the right thing at just the right time.

At work, Promoters are so likable and **charming** with customers and clients that they almost seem to have depths of sympathy, when actually they are reading people's faces and **observing** their tone of voice and body language. Promoters keep their eyes open and their ears cocked, always scanning for signs of assent or dissent, always alert to the tiniest cues that give away people's attitudes, and with **nerves of steel** they will use this information to make a sale or close a deal.

Naturally **daring**, and ever-**optimistic** that things will go their way, Promoters want to have new **experiences**, want to be where the **action** is, and seem exhilarated by skating close to the edge of disaster. In fact, a theme of seeking **excitement** through taking **risks**, in work and in play, runs throughout their lives.

While they are often surrounded by people, Promoters rarely let anyone get really close to them, and so are usually something of a **puzzle** to others. Promoters understand well the maxim, "He who travels fastest, travels alone"—although they are not likely to be alone for long, since their **boldness** and sense of **adventure** make them highly attractive to many other people.

Film Portrait: Jerry Maguire (Tom Cruise) in *Jerry Maguire*

Crafters (ISTP)

Like all Artisans, Crafters love physical action, but their specialty is in working with **tools** and **equipment** of all kinds, not only hand tools used in the building trades, but also vehicles, weapons, machines, sports equipment, and musical instruments of all types. Crafters (between 5-7% of the population) are the true masters of tools, able to handle them with an **artistry** that defies belief.

Although Crafters are driven to master whatever tools call to them, they do not really practice with their tools, but **play** with them impulsively, on the spur of the moment, when the urge strikes them. Crafters also seek fun and games on **impulse**, looking for any **opportunity** to play around with their many **toys**: cars, motorcycles, boats, dune buggies, hunting rifles, fishing tackle, scuba gear, and on and on.

Crafters thrive on **excitement**, especially the rush of **speed** found in drag racing, skiing, motocross biking, surfing, etc. In all of these activities, they are **fearless**, always pushing the limits of their ability, exposing themselves to **danger** again and again, even despite frequent injury. Of all the types, Crafters are most likely to be **risk-takers**, pitting themselves against disaster.

Crafters are hard to get to know, probably because they tend to communicate through **action**, and show little interest in developing verbal skills. Their silence can **isolate** them at school and on the job, and even when they hang around with their friends they base their companionship on their tool **skills**, letting their actions speak for them, and keeping their conversation sparse and brief. This disinterest in language can also make Crafters appear lost in the classroom, and teachers can even think they're slow learners, although this is usually misleading. Crafters might not be book-smart, but they are **street-smart**, savvy, and gifted with their **senses**, especially with their hands and eyes. So while they often ignore their school work, they will work for hours on end doing whatever interests them.

Crafters are typically **generous** with their friends, often volunteering to help with projects—house remodeling, for example, or working on cars or boats. At the same time, they resent being tied down or told what to do, and they regard rules and regulations as a straightjacket. Crafters will not usually defy authority openly and fight the establishment, but will simply and **silently** go their own way. More than anything, Crafters want to do their own thing, and they do their best work when they have the **freedom** to explore their craft in their own way, and on their own time.

Film Portrait: Roy Hobbs (Robert Redford) in *The Natural*

Performers (ESFP)

Performers are **entertainers** at heart who love to put on a show for others. Whether at work or with friends and family, Performers are **high-energy** and full of **fun**, and they live with a **theatrical** flourish that makes even the most routine events seem **exciting**. Happy whenever they can find an **audience**, and often greatly talented in music, comedy, and acting, Performers are the people for whom it can truly be said "all the world's a stage."

Performers are plentiful (right around 10% of the population), and a good thing, because their great talent lies in showing the rest of us how to lighten up and **enjoy** ourselves. Because they're so **playful** and **colorful**—the life of the party—Performers are usually well liked, quickly becoming the center of **attention** wherever they are. In fact, Performers really aren't comfortable being alone, and whenever possible they'll seek the **company** of others, which they usually find, for they make wonderful playmates and partygoers.

Talkative and **witty**, Performers always seem to know the latest jokes and stories, and are quick with wisecracks and wordplay—nothing is so serious or sacred that it can't be joked about. Performers also like to live in the **fast lane**, and are often eager to try out the "in" nightclub, the chic new fashion, and the hot new band.

The Performers' "eat, drink, and be merry" attitude is healthy for the most part, although it also makes them dangerously **vulnerable** to substance abuse. **Pleasure** seems to be an end in itself for them, and **variety** is the spice of life. And so Performers will try almost anything that looks like fun, or that stimulates their **senses**, not always giving enough thought to the consequences.

Like the other Artisans, Performers are born **optimists**—"Always look on the bright side," is their motto—and they will avoid worries and troubles by ignoring them as long as possible. They're also **affectionate** people, and are probably the most **generous** of all the types. Without a mean or stingy bone in their body—what's theirs is yours—Performers seem to have little idea of saving or conserving. They give what they have to one and all, just as they love **freely**, without expecting anything in return. In so many ways, Performers see life as a **cornucopia** overflowing with life's pleasures.

Film Portrait: Guido Orefice (Roberto Benigni) in *Life is Beautiful*

Composers (ISFP)

Composers do not only write music, but they make all kinds of **artistic** forms. While the other Artisans are talented with people, tools, and entertainments, Composers are closely in tune with their five **senses**, and so have an exceptional ability—seemingly inborn—to work and play in their compositions with the subtlest **differences** in color, tone, texture, aroma, and flavor.

Composers are nearly as numerous as the other Artisans (around 5-7% of the population), but in general they are very difficult to observe and are greatly **misunderstood**, most likely because they tend not to express themselves verbally, preferring to put aside words in order to **live** more fully in their senses. Make no mistake, Composers are just as interested as other types in sharing their views of the world, and some will express themselves eloquently through their **artistry**. But even many successful Composers remain virtually unknown to the world at large, their quietness leaving them all but **invisible** to others.

Although Composers often put in long, lonely hours into their works of art, they are just as **impulsive** and **playful** as the other Artisans. They do not wait to consider their moves; rather, they act **spontaneously**, in the here and now, when the urge hits them, with little or no planning or preparation. Composers are **seized by the act** of artistic creation as if caught up in a whirlwind. The act is their master, and they are driven to obey. Composers paint or sculpt, write melodies, design clothes, create new recipes—or whatever—simply because they must.

Captured in this way by their physical actions, **excited** and **absorbed** in their art, Composers seem oblivious to the fatigue and pain involved in their work. And yet they are especially sensitive to the suffering of others, and they do a great deal of **philanthropic** work to help alleviate people's misfortune and distress.

Some Composers have a remarkable way with young **children**, almost as if there were a natural bond of **sympathy** and trust between them. Composers can have a similar bond with animals, even **wild animals**, and many have an instinctive fondness for the outdoors.

Film Portrait: Wolfgang Amadeus Mozart (Tom Hulce) in *Amadeus*

Four Guardians

Guardians, don't forget, are the *cornerstone* temperament, the administrators and conservators of institutions who most often speak about *what is* and who try to do *what's right*. But Guardians also have some fundamental differences in how and where they go about their business.

Supervisors (ESTJ)

There are a good many Supervisors (around 12-15% of the population), and we should be grateful, for they are the pillars of their community—the **dependable** and **trustworthy** people who uphold the institutions of civilized life.

Supervisors are **outgoing** and community-minded, and very often belong to a number of **service** clubs, lodges, and associations. Supervisors also give a great deal of their time and energy to school, church, or community **groups**, supporting them through **steady** attendance, with many rising to positions of leadership.

Supervisors have an innate respect for **authority**. As children they look up to and obey their parents, and in school they are often model students, **dutifully** following directions and doing all of their assignments. Above all else, little Supervisors wish to do what's expected of them, and they rarely question a parent or teacher's instructions, standards, or authority. And they show these same qualities as they grow into adulthood and take on the **responsibilities** of job and family.

At work, Supervisors enjoy and are good at making **schedules**, agendas, inventories, and so on, and they put their trust in **tried and true** ways of doing things. Supervisors keep their feet firmly on the ground, and they would like those in their charge to do the same, whether employee, subordinate, spouse, or offspring. Supervisors naturally take **control** of groups and are comfortable issuing **orders**, which they expect to be obeyed. They are **cooperative** with their own superiors, and they would like cooperation from the people working under them. **Rank**, they believe, has its obligations, but it also has its privileges. Supervisors have no problem evaluating others and tend to judge how a person is doing in terms of his or her **compliance** with, and **respect** for, schedules and procedures.

Supervisors approach social and family life along **traditional** lines. They make **loyal** spouses and **conscientious** parents, and they tend to have a large circle of friends, with some of their most valuable **friendships** dating back many years. They enjoy **social** gatherings and ceremonies, and they look forward to holiday parties, club dances, weddings, class reunions, awards banquets, and so on. In social situations, Supervisors speak easily with their friends, and often express strong opinions on social and **political** issues. Although they can seem a bit formal in their manners, they are pretty easy to get to know—what they seem to be, they are.

Film Portrait: Colonel Nicholson (Alec Guinness) in *The Bridge on the River Kwai*

Inspectors (ISTJ)

The one word that best describes Inspectors is "**superdependable**." Whether at home or at work, Inspectors are remarkably earnest and **reliable**, particularly when it comes to keeping an eye on the people and products they're responsible for. In their **quiet** way, Inspectors work hard to make sure that rules are followed, laws are respected, and standards are upheld.

Inspectors (something like 7 or 8% of the population) are the true backbone of **institutions**. They are patient with their work and with the procedures within an institution, although not always with the unauthorized behavior of some people in that institution. **Responsible** to the core, Inspectors like it when people know their duties, follow the guidelines, and operate within the **rules**. For their part, Inspectors will see to it that goods are examined and **schedules** are kept, that resources will be up to **standards** and delivered when and where they are supposed to be. And they would prefer that everyone be this **trustworthy**.

Inspectors can be **hard-nosed** about the need for following the rules in the workplace, and do not hesitate to report irregularities to the proper **authorities**. Because of this they are often misjudged as being hardhearted, for people fail to see their good intentions and their vulnerability to criticism. Also, because they usually make their inspections without much flourish or fanfare, the **dedication** Inspectors bring to their duties can go unnoticed and unappreciated.

While not as talkative as Supervisor Guardians, Inspectors are still highly **sociable**, and are likely to be involved (though usually behind the scenes) in community service organizations, such as Sunday School, Little League, or Scouting, that transmit **traditional** values to the young. Like all Guardians, Inspectors hold dear their **family** ceremonies—weddings, birthdays, and anniversaries—although they tend to be uncomfortable if the occasion becomes too large or too public.

Generally speaking, Inspectors are not comfortable with anything that gets too fancy. Their words tend to be plain and **down-to-earth**, their clothes are often simple and **conservative**, and their homes and workplaces are usually neat and clean and **modest**. As for personal property, such as cars or home appliances, Inspectors usually choose **sensible** standard models over those loaded with expensive new features, and they will often try to find sound, well-cared for used items—they even hunt for classics and antiques—preferring the **old-fashioned** to the newfangled every time.

Film Portrait: Rose Sayer (Katherine Hepburn) in *The African Queen*

Providers (ESFJ)

Providers take it upon themselves to provide for the **welfare** of their families, students, employees, and so on, but they are also the most **sociable** of all the Guardians, and thus are the great contributors to social **institutions** such as schools, churches, social clubs, and civic groups. Providers are numerous (12-15% of the population), and this is fortunate for the rest of us, because social **service** is the key to their nature. Wherever they go, Providers **give** happily of their time and energy to make sure that the needs of others are met, and that social functions are a success.

Hard working themselves, Providers are good at getting people to pitch in and help on social occasions, and they are also tireless in their attention to the **details** of goods and services. They make excellent chairpersons in charge of dances, banquets, class reunions, charity fund-raisers, and the like. They are without peer as masters of **ceremonies**, able to speak publicly with ease and confidence. And they are outstanding **hosts**, knowing everyone by name, and seemingly aware of what everyone's been doing. Providers enjoy entertaining, and are always **concerned** that their guests are well provided for.

Providers are **gregarious** and can become restless when isolated from people. They like to **talk** with others, and will even strike up a conversation with strangers and chat pleasantly about any topic that comes to mind. Providers also show a delightful fascination with news of their friends and neighbors, and they love to gossip about what's been going on in the local community, school, or church. **Friendships** matter a great deal to Providers, and while they are perhaps the most **sympathetic** of all the types, they are also somewhat self-conscious, that is, concerned about what their friends think of them. Loving and **affectionate** themselves, they need to be loved and appreciated in return.

Providers take their role as **family** provider seriously, in both a material and a moral sense. They try to make sure their family has a comfortable home, healthy food, clean clothes, and a **sensible** store of possessions. They are **responsible** about home repairs and yard work, they like the house neat and tidy, and they are conscientious, even **sentimental**, about observing family **traditions** such as birthdays and anniversaries.

In addition, Providers have a strong set of family **values** with clear "shoulds" and "shouldn'ts," which they expect their family members to abide by. Providers want family issues settled quickly and with little fuss, and they want family life run according to **schedule** and with respect for the **rules**.

Film Portrait: Edna Spalding (Sally Field) in *Places in the Heart*

Protectors (ISFJ)

We are lucky that Protectors are so numerous (say 7 or 8% the population), because their primary interest is in the **safety** and **security** of those they care about—their family, their circle of friends, their students, their patients, their boss, their fellow workers, or their employees. Protectors have an extraordinary sense of **loyalty** in their makeup, and seem fulfilled by shielding others from the difficulties of life.

Speculating and experimenting do not particularly interest Protectors, who prefer to make do with **time-honored** products and procedures rather than change to new. At work Protectors are seldom happy in situations where the rules are constantly changing, or where long-established ways of doing things are not respected. At bottom, Protectors value **tradition**, not only in their jobs, but also in their society and in their family. Protectors believe deeply in the **stability** of social ranking conferred by birth, titles, offices, and credentials. They also cherish family **history** and enjoy caring for family **property**, from homesteads to heirlooms.

Wanting to be of **service** to others, Protectors find great satisfaction in assisting the downtrodden, and can deal with disability and neediness in others better than any other type. They tend to be reserved and quiet in manner, and their **shyness** is often misjudged as stiffness, even coldness, when in truth Protectors are **warm-hearted** and **sympathetic**, giving happily of themselves to those in need.

Their reserve ought really to be seen as an expression of their **sincerity** and **seriousness** of purpose. The most **industrious** of all the types, Protectors are willing to work long hours, quietly doing all the thankless jobs that others manage to escape. Protectors are quite happy to work alone; in fact, they aren't that comfortable in charge of people, and may try to do everything themselves rather than tell others to get the job done. **Thoroughness** and **frugality** are also virtues for them. When Protectors undertake a task, they will complete it if humanly possible. They also know better than any other type the value of a dollar. To **save**, to put something aside for a rainy day, to **insure** against disasters—these are actions near and dear to the Protector's heart.

For all these reasons, Protectors are frequently **overworked**, just as they are frequently misunderstood and **undervalued**. Their contributions, and also their economies, are often taken for granted, and they rarely get the appreciation they deserve.

Film Portrait: Will Kane (Gary Cooper) in *High Noon*

Four Idealists

Idealists, let me remind you, are the *personal growth* temperament, the mentors and personal advocates who most often speak about *what's possible* and who try to do *what's right*. But Idealists also have some essential differences in how and where they influence the people around them.

Teachers (ENFJ)

More than all the other types, more even than the other Idealists, Teachers are born **educators**, with a natural talent for helping people learn about the world and explore their talents.

Teachers (about 5% of the population) are gifted at **dreaming** up fascinating lessons for their students. In some Teachers this ability—effortless, it seems, and almost endless—to fire the **imagination** can amount to a kind of creative genius. But just as important is their belief in each student's **potential**. Teachers look for the best in their students, making it clear that each one has a world of promise. And this **positive** energy can affect their students greatly, making them want to live up to these expectations, and so **inspiring** them to grow and develop more than they ever thought possible.

Teachers are remarkably good with language, especially when **communicating** person-to-person. Warmly exuberant, often bubbling with **enthusiasm**, Teachers do not hesitate to speak out and let their feelings be known. Often they will voice their passions with **dramatic** flourish, and they can, with practice, become exceptional public speakers. This speaking ability gives Teachers a good deal of **influence** in groups, and they are often asked to take a **leadership** role in their school or business.

In whatever field they choose, Teachers consider **people** their highest priority, and they excel in almost any activity where close human **contact** is involved. Teachers have great **insight** into people; they know what's going on inside themselves, and they can read others with uncanny accuracy. Teachers also **identify** with others quite easily, and will actually find themselves picking up some of the characteristics and emotions they see in those around them.

Because they slip almost unconsciously into other people's skin in this way, Teachers feel closely **connected** with those around them, and thus show a **personal** concern for others, and a **sincere** interest in the joys and problems of their employees, colleagues, students, clients, and loved ones.

Teachers like things settled and **decided**, and will schedule their work hours and social engagements well ahead of time. And they can be counted on to honor these commitments. Valuing as they do social **cooperation** and **harmonious** personal relations, Teachers are extraordinarily tolerant of others, and are strongly committed to **justice** and fair play for the people close to them—in fact, for people everywhere.

Film Portrait: John Keating (Robin Williams) in *Dead Poets Society*

Counselors (INFJ)

Counselors have a strong desire to contribute to the welfare of others, and they find great fulfillment interacting with people, nurturing their personal **development** and guiding them along a journey of **self-discovery**.

Counselors are scarce (2-3% of the population), and can be hard to get to know, since they tend to share their innermost thoughts and feelings only with their loved ones. They are highly **private** people, with unusually rich, **complicated** inner lives. Friends or colleagues who have known a Counselor for years are likely to see new sides emerging, as the Counselor's personal journey winds its way through life. Not that Counselors are flighty or scattered. On the contrary, they value their **integrity** a great deal; but they have **mysterious**, intricately woven personalities which sometimes puzzle even them.

Blessed with vivid **imaginations**, Counselors are often seen as the most **poetical** of all the types, and they do feature a lot of poetic imagery and lyrical metaphors in their everyday language. More interested in inspiration than information, Counselors use their great talent for language—both written and spoken—to communicate their **passionate** feelings and their **personal** insights.

Although they are happy working at tasks (such as reading and writing) that require **solitude** and close attention, Counselors do quite well with individuals or groups of people, provided that their professional relationships are not superficial, and that they can find some quiet, alone time every now and then to recharge their batteries. Counselors are great **listeners** and seem naturally interested in helping people with their personal problems. Counselors are highly **intuitive** and can recognize another's emotions or intentions—good or evil—even before that person is aware of them. Counselors themselves can seldom tell how they came to read others' feelings so keenly. This uncanny **insight** into others could very well be the basis of the Counselor's remarkable ability to experience a whole array of **psychic** phenomena.

Counselors also tend to work effectively in organizations. They value staff **harmony**, are good at consulting and **cooperating** with others, and usually find argument or debate disagreeable and destructive. Counselors are deeply concerned with people's **feelings** about each other, and about the organization, and they insist on treating everyone—above them or below them—**justly**, fairly, and with respect. Not usually visible leaders, Counselors prefer to work **intensely** with those close to them, especially on a one-to-one basis, quietly exerting their **influence** behind the scenes.

Film Portrait: Malcolm Crowe (Bruce Willis) in *The Sixth Sense*

Champions (ENFP)

Like the other Idealists, there aren't many Champions (no more than 5% of the population), but even more than the others they consider powerful **emotional** experiences as being vital to a full life. Champions have a wide range and variety of emotions, and a great passion for **exploration**. They see life as an exciting drama, pregnant with possibilities for both good and evil, and they want to seek out and experience all the **meaningful** events and fascinating people in the world.

The most outgoing and **talkative** of the Idealists, Champions often can't wait to tell others of their extraordinary experiences. Champions can be **effervescent** when talking with others, like fountains that bubble and splash, spilling over their own words to get it all out. And usually this is not simple storytelling; Champions often speak (or write) in the hope of revealing some **truth** about human experience, or of motivating others with their **fervent** convictions. Their strong drive to speak out on issues and events, along with their boundless **enthusiasm** and natural talent with language, makes them the most **inspiring** of all the types.

Fiercely **individualistic**, Champions strive toward a kind of personal **authenticity**, and this intention always to be themselves is usually quite attractive to people. At the same time, Champions have outstanding **intuitive** powers and can tell what's going on inside of others, reading hidden emotions and giving special significance to words or actions.

In fact, Champions are constantly **watching** the people around them, and no quirk of character or hidden motive is likely to escape their attention. Far more than the other Idealists, Champions are **keen** observers of people, and are capable of intense concentration on another individual. Their attention is rarely passive or casual. On the contrary, Champions tend to be extra **alert**, always on the lookout for what's **possible**.

Champions are great with people and usually have a wide range of close personal relationships. They are **warm** and full of **fun**—even somewhat **mischievous**—with their friends and colleagues, and they handle their employees or students with great skill. They are comfortable in public and on the telephone, and are so **imaginative** and **high-spirited** that others love to be in their company. Champions are **positive**, passionate people, and often their confidence in the goodness of life and of human nature makes good things happen.

Film Portrait: Katie Morosky (Barbra Streisand) in *The Way We Were*

Healers (INFP)

Healers present a calm and **serene** face to the world, and can seem shy, even distant around other people. In their feelings, however, they're anything but distant, having a capacity for personal **caring** that's rare even for Idealists. Healers care deeply about their own **inner life**, and that of their loved ones, but also about important

causes in the world at large. And their great passion is to heal the conflicts that plague people, or that divide groups, and thus to bring **wholeness** to themselves, their family, and their community.

Set off from the rest of humanity by their quietness and scarcity (around 2-3% of the population), Healers can feel even more alone in the **intensity** of their idealism. Healers have a **fervent** sense of idealism that comes from a strong personal sense of right and wrong. They conceive of the world as an **ethical**, honorable place, full of wondrous **possibilities** and potential goods. In fact, to understand Healers, we must understand that their deep commitment to the **positive** and the good is almost boundless and selfless, **inspiring** them to make extraordinary **sacrifices** for someone or something they believe in.

Also, Healers might well feel a sense of separation because of their often misunderstood childhood. Healers typically live a quiet, **fantasy-filled** childhood—they are the prince or princess of fairy tales—an attitude which, sadly, is frowned upon, or even punished, by many parents. With parents who want their children to get their head out of the clouds, Healers can begin to believe they are bad to be so **fanciful**, so **dreamy**, and can come to see themselves as ugly ducklings. In truth, they are quite OK just as they are, only different from most others—swans reared in a family of ducks.

At work, Healers are agreeable and **cooperative**, welcoming new ideas and new information. They are patient with complicated situations, but impatient with routine details. Healers are also highly **intuitive**, keenly aware of people and their feelings, and they relate well with most others. Because of their deep-seated **reserve**, however, they can work quite happily alone.

When making decisions, Healers follow their **heart**, which means they can make errors of fact, but seldom of **feeling**. They have a natural interest in scholarly activities and demonstrate, like the other Idealists, a remarkable facility with **language**. They have a gift for interpreting **stories**, as well as for creating them, and thus often write in lyric, **poetic** fashion. Frequently they hear a **call** to go forth into the world and help others, a call they seem ready to answer, even if they must sacrifice their own comfort.

Film Portrait: Tom Joad (Henry Fonda) in *The Grapes of Wrath*

Four Rationals

Rationals, if you recall, are the *technology* temperament, the project coordinators and engineers who most often speak about *what's possible* and who look to do *what works*. But Rationals also have some significant differences in how and where they make their plans.

Fieldmarshals (ENTJ)

From an early age Fieldmarshals can be observed taking **command** of groups, so instinctive is their **leadership** ability. Sometimes they wonder why they always seem to be in charge of people and projects. But the reason is simply that the basic, driving force of Fieldmarshals is to mobilize personnel and resources in preparation for launching major **enterprises** and **campaigns**.

Although Fieldmarshals are just as rare as the other Rationals, (no more than 2-3% of the population), their talent for **strategic** command has given them widespread influence. They make superb **executives** for any organization, whether in the military, business, education, or government. Fieldmarshals **visualize** where the organization is going, keeping both short-term and long-range **objectives** well in mind. They are exceptionally good at **communicating** their vision to their personnel. And they're best of all the Rationals at getting operations up and running and at **coordinating** forces in the field.

Fieldmarshals are the supreme **pragmatists**, always aware of the relationship of means to ends, always looking to bring **order** and **efficiency** to their organizations. **Ingenious** in pursuit of their goals, they will plot out every step needed to achieve their objective, and will instantly and permanently eliminate all unnecessary steps from the plan of operations. For Fieldmarshals, there must always be a good **reason** for doing anything, and they insist that their decisions be based on objective **data** and a well thought-out **rationale**.

More than any other type, Fieldmarshals are skilled at **reducing bureaucracy** in any of its forms. While they will tolerate some established procedures that work well, they can and will abandon any procedure that is shown to be inefficient or ineffective, quickly reassigning their people to more productive actions. **Tough-minded** and **decisive**, Fieldmarshals are willing to dismiss employees who cannot shake off old routines and increase their **productivity**. They are particularly impatient with incompetence, and repeating errors drives them crazy.

Sometimes referred to as the "leader of leaders," Fieldmarshals use all of their skills—arranging priorities, compiling evidence, demonstrating ideas, issuing orders—in an effort to build smoothly functioning **systems**. But they have to be careful, for they can push toward their goals with such tireless, **single-minded** drive that they can steamroll their loved ones and shortchange other areas of life.

Film Portrait: Douglas MacArthur (Gregory Peck) in *MacArthur*

Masterminds (INTJ)

All Rationals are good at **planning** operations, but Masterminds are head and shoulders above all the rest at **contingency** planning. Any complex operation involves many stages, one following another in a necessary progression, and Masterminds are easily able to grasp how each step leads to the next. But problems can arise any step along the way, and strategic plans need to include options to overcome these hurdles and stay on target. Here Masterminds excel, never setting off on their current project without a Plan A firmly in mind, but always ready to switch to Plan B—or C, or D, if need be.

Masterminds are really rare (maybe 1-2% of the population), and they are rarely encountered outside their office, factory, school, or laboratory. Although they can be highly **capable** leaders, Masterminds are not looking to take command, and will usually stay in the **background** until others prove their inability to lead.

Once they take charge, however, they are thoroughgoing **pragmatists**. Masterminds are certain that **efficiency** is the basis of a well-run organization, and if they encounter inefficiency—any waste of human and material resources—they are quick to realign operations and to reassign personnel. Strongly **independent** in their thinking, Masterminds do not feel bound by established rules and procedures, and traditional authority does not impress them, nor do slogans or catchwords. Only ideas that **make sense** to them are adopted; those that don't, aren't, no matter who thought of them. Remember, their aim is always maximum efficiency.

Solving problems and figuring out puzzles is great fun for Masterminds, who love responding to tangled systems that require **ingenious** thinking and the careful sorting out of **factors**. In careers requiring these skills, Masterminds usually rise to positions of responsibility, for they work long and hard, and are **dedicated** in their pursuit of goals, sparing neither their own time and effort nor that of their colleagues and employees. Although **tough** with their people, Masterminds are also a **positive** force in the workplace, preferring to comment on people's successes and not their errors. They are more interested in moving an organization forward than dwelling on mistakes.

Masterminds tend to be much more **definite** and **self-confident** than other Rationals, having usually developed a clear **vision** of their objectives and strong **opinions** on how to proceed. Decisions come easily to them; in fact, they can hardly rest until they have things settled and **decided**. But before they make up their mind, they must do the **research**. Masterminds insist on looking at all available **data** before they decide on a course of action, and they are suspicious of any move that is based on shoddy research, or that is not checked against reality.

Film Portrait: Jane Craig (Holly Hunter) in *Broadcast News*

Inventors (ENTP)

Inventors begin building gadgets and mechanisms as young children, and never really stop, although as adults they will turn their inventiveness to many kinds of organizations, social as well as technological. Inventors are few and far between (only 2-3% of the population), but they have great impact on our everyday lives. With their **innovative** spirit, Inventors are always on the lookout for a better way, always pondering new **methods**, always exploring new **enterprises**.

Inventors are keenly **pragmatic**, and often become expert at devising the most **efficient** ways and means to accomplish their goals. They are the most reluctant of all the types to do something in a particular manner just because that's the way it's been done before. As a result, they often bring **ingenious** new approaches to their work and play. They are intensely **curious** and will **probe** continuously for alternatives and **possibilities**, especially when trying to solve complex problems.

Inventors are always coming up with new **ideas**, but they most value ideas that make possible actions and products. They see technological design not as an end in itself, but as a means to an end, as a way of devising the **prototype** that works and that can be brought to **market**. Inventors count on their ability to solve problems as they arise, and don't usually make a detailed blueprint in advance. A rough idea is all they need to feel ready to get to work.

Inventors are usually **nonconformists** in the workplace, and can succeed in many areas as long as the job does not involve too much humdrum routine. They make good leaders on pilot projects that test their **creativity**. And they are good at **organizing** human systems, quickly grasping the **politics** of institutions and making every effort to **understand** the people within the system rather than order them around. No matter what their occupation, Inventors display an extraordinary talent for rising to the demands of even the most impossible situations. "It can't be done" only **challenges** the Inventor to reply, "I can do it."

Inventors often have a lively circle of friends and are interested in their ideas and activities. They are usually **easygoing**, seldom critical or carping. And they can be fascinating conversationalists, able to express their own **complicated** ideas and to follow the ideas of others. But be warned: when arguing issues, Inventors are **competitive** and need to maintain a one-up position on their opponents.

Film Portrait: Preston Tucker (Jeff Bridges) in *Tucker: The Man and His Dream*

Architects (INTP)

Architects should not be thought of as only interested in drawing blueprints for bridges and buildings. They are also the architects of **ideas**, designing all kinds of **theoretical** systems, including educational curricula, corporate strategies, political ideologies, philosoph-

135

ical treatises, mathematical arguments, and scientific experiments.

Architects are rare (around 1-2% of the population) and are often difficult to know. They are inclined to be **reserved** except with close friends, and their privacy is difficult to penetrate. Able to **concentrate** better than any other type, they prefer to work quietly, and often alone, in their labs or at their computers and drafting tables. Architects also become **obsessed** with **systems** analysis, and this can seem to shut others out. Once wrapped up in a thought process, Architects close off from people and work until they comprehend the issue they're considering in all its **complexity**.

For Architects, the world exists primarily to be **analyzed**, understood, and explained. External reality in itself is unimportant, merely an arena for checking out the usefulness of ideas. What's important for Architects is that they uncover the underlying **structures** of the universe, and that their statements about how the world works are accurate, **logical**, and comprehensive. **Curiosity** about these fundamental structures is the driving force in Architects, and they care little if others understand or accept their ideas. Unfortunately, they can seem **arrogant** in their grand desire to grasp and to articulate the universe, and they may show impatience with others who have less **ingenuity** or less drive.

Ruthless **pragmatists** about ideas, Architects will learn in any manner and degree they can. They are **independent**-minded and will listen to amateurs if their ideas are useful, and will ignore the experts if theirs are not. Authority derived from office, credential, or celebrity does not impress them. Architects are interested only in what make **sense**—and thus only statements that are **consistent** and **coherent** carry any weight with them.

Architects show the greatest **precision** in thought and speech of all the types. They tend to see distinctions and inconsistencies instantly, and can detect contradictions in any argument. It is difficult for an Architect to listen to nonsense, even in a casual conversation, and in any serious discussion they can be devastating, their skill in logic and **debate** giving them an enormous advantage. Architects regard all discussions as a search for **understanding**, and they believe their function is to eliminate inconsistencies, which can make communication with them an uncomfortable experience for many.

Film Portrait: Howard Roark (Gary Cooper) in *The Fountainhead*

About the Author...

Dr. Stephen Montgomery (a Counselor Idealist) is an award winning teacher, a National Endowment for the Humanities fellow, and a consultant for the Educational Testing Service. As David Keirsey's research assistant and editor, and as his son-in-law, Montgomery has studied temperament theory up close and personal with Dr. Keirsey for more than twenty years. He has been married to Keirsey's daughter, Janene (a Mastermind Rational), for over thirty-four years. They are the proud parents of twin sons about to graduate from college and to begin careers in creative writing and astro physics. Dr. Montgomery's other works in temperament studies consist of a series on the four temperaments in love and marriage called *The Pygmalion Project.*

Prometheus Nemesis Book Company
Short Order Form

Qty $0.00

• *Please Understand Me II* Keirsey   346 pages—$15.95
An update of *Please Understand Me*. Presents Keirsey's latest ideas on differences in temperament and character in mating, parenting, leading, and SmartWork™. Comprehensive discussions of Artisans, Guardians, Idealists, & Rationals, and the 16 personality types.

• *Leadership, Temperament, and Talent* Keirsey   40 pages—$ 5.00
Edited from *Please Understand Me II*. Examines four different leaders making use of four different kinds of talent—tactical, logistical, diplomatic, strategic. Helpful for personnel placement, management training, and career counseling.

• *The Sixteen Types* Keirsey   48 pages—$5.00
Portraits of all sixteen personality types, edted from *Please Understand Me II*. Plus *The Keirsey Temperament Sorter II* & *The Keirsey FourTypes Sorter*.

• *The Keirsey Temperament Sorter II* $.50
Self-scoring questionnaire designed to identify the sixteen personality types, reprinted from *Please Understand Me II*.

• *Please Understand Me, The Videotape*   75 Minutes—$19.95
Illustrates many of the character traits of the Artisans, Guardians, Idealists, and Rationals. Uses current and historical footage, comments from Keirsey, and type interviews to show the impact of temperament and character styles in mating, management, and education.

• *Please Understand Me* Keirsey & Bates   208 pages—$11.95
National Best Seller. Two million copies sold. A 40 year clinical study of four types of temperament as they differ in mating, parenting, and leading.

• *The Pygmalion Project: 1 The Artisan* Montgomery   180 pages—$9.95
The impulsive Artisan style of love with Guardians, Rationals, and Idealists, as illustrated by characters in stories and films.

• *The Pygmalion Project: 2 The Guardian* Montgomery 258 pages—$9.95
The responsible Guardian style of love with Artisans, Idealists, and Rationals, as illustrated by characters in stories and films.

• *The Pygmalion Project: 3 The Idealist* Montgomery 325 pages—$11.95
The soulful Idealist style of love with Artisans, Guardians, and Rationals, as illustrated by characters in stories and films.

• *People Patterns* Montgomery   136 pages—$11.95
A modern guide to the four temperaments. Uses characters from popular books, movies, music, and TV—from *Harry Potter* to *Star Trek*, from the Beatles to *Sex and the City*—to bring the Artisans, Guardians, Idealists, and Rationals alive for a contemporary audience. Includes a new short form **personality sorter** and chapters on dating and mating, on parents and their children, and on choosing the right career path.

Total Enclosed [   ]

Name _____

Address _____

City _____ State ____ Zip _____

For arrival of order before four weeks call 800-754-0039 for UPS shipping charges. Mail order and check (US Dollars only) to PN Books, Box 2748, Del Mar, CA 92014. 760-632-1575; Fax 858-481-0535 or Fax 714-540-5288

Subtotal _____

7.75% Sales Tax (CA Only) _____

Shipping _____

Shipping Charges

Order Subtotal	USA	Abroad
$ 00.00 - $ 29.99 —	$3.00	$ 6.00
30.00 - 59.99 —	5.00	10.00
60.00 - 99.99 —	7.00	15.00
100.00 - 149.99 —	10.00	30.00
over $150 call for charges		